Spartanburg County
A PICTORIAL HISTORY

Spartanburg County
A PICTORIAL HISTORY

Philip N. Racine

**Designed by
Jamie Backus**

**Donning Company/Publishers
Virginia Beach, Virginia**

The Donning Company/Publishers, 5041 Admiral Wright
Road, Virginia Beach, Virginia 23462.

Library of Congress Cataloging in Publication Data:

Racine, Philip N.
    Spartanburg: a pictorial history.

1. Spartanburg, S.C.—History   2. Spartanburg, S.C.—
Description.   I. Title
F279.S7R3   975.7'29   80-20869
ISBN 0-89865-051-8 (pbk.)

4

For Lewis P. Jones,
who suggested it,
and to the memory of my Father,
who would have enjoyed it.

Contents

Foreword

The history of Spartanburg County is recorded in several books, but it has never been compiled in photographs. Photographs bring us moments in history that tell of their time in ways that words cannot. This collection of photographs illustrates the county's rich history. It shows the ways in which the area has been part of the peculiar history of the South and the ways in which it has been affected by and has contributed to the history of the nation. Spartanburg County's agricultural as well as her industrial history is illustrated here, and her population of city and rural dwellers, textile workers and farmers, whites and blacks all make silent statements. A collection of photographs, taken over time, reveals much about change in the county, but more importantly, it tells us about the people who lived here. The story needs telling in this special way, and the Spartanburg County Historical Association welcomes this effort.

Frank Cunningham, president
Spartanburg County Historical Association

Variously known as Nicholl's Fort, Tanner's Mill, and Anderson's Mill, this structure sits on a foundation which dates from about 1780. The first court in the county met here in 1785. The water mill continued operation into the 1970s. It is located southeast of the city of Spartanburg where SC-64 crosses the North Tyger River.

Photograph by James Buchanan; courtesy of the Spartanburg County Historical Association.

Introduction

This book is divided into three general sections. The first section relates the history of the county to 1880, covering a time when the village and county were frontier; the second section examines a period (1880 to 1920) when agriculture, the cotton-textile industry, the railroads, and the city itself grew and changed significantly; and the third section (from 1920 to the present) chronicles depression and disillusionment followed by amazing recovery. Such a division places the bulk of the photographs in the second section, during the years from 1880 to 1920, largely because that is the time when photographs became available, and it seemed important to emphasize the past at the possible expense of more recent times.

Within each of the general sections the photographs are arranged roughly according to decades. The arrangement is only approximately chronological because the intent is to give some feeling for what it was like to live at a certain time. If some form of entertainment pictured in 1908 is like another pictured in 1904, these photographs belong together. In general, the nature of the available photographs determined the thrust of the book; much that was important in the history of the county is not chronicled here. Lastly, the narrative is longer for the earlier history because visual material for that time is scarce.

In a very important way this book is a joint effort. Linda Taylor Hudgins took torn, faded, and wrinkled pictures and turned them into the photographs you see here. For that minor miracle I am grateful. She worked diligently, met her deadlines, and took pride in her work. Thanks are also due all the people who shared their treasures with me. Special thanks to Lionel Lawson, William B. Littlejohn, Alice Brown, Marion P. Holt, James Harrison, Herbert Hucks, Frank Cunningham, and Martha Mathews. At critical junctures both my wife, Frances Melton Racine, and my friend Richard B. Harwell made this book possible.

Philip N. Racine
Wofford College

Charles Moore began building Walnut Grove in 1765 on land granted him by King George III. Moore emigrated from the north of Ireland to Pennsylvania and then to Spartanburg in the early 1760s. He received several grants which amounted to about three thousand acres. His land, located on the Tyger River about ten miles south of the village, has been controlled by his family ever since. The house, restored in the 1960s, was one of the nicest in the county in the eighteenth century. It should be remembered, however, that this was a working farm and was probably not in as pristine a condition as it appears in this photograph.

Photograph by B & B Studio.

Eighteenth Century to 1880

White men who came to the South Carolina back country in the early eighteenth century found few Indians living in the Spartanburg area. When they did find them, the Indians were hostile. Not until much later did whites discover that the Spartanburg area was a favorite Cherokee hunting ground and that the presence of whites constituted a threat to the Indians' source of food and clothing. At some time in the past Indians had inhabited the area, for they had burned the underbrush and many of the trees to provide growing areas for their crops. When the whites arrived they found fields, meadows, hardwoods, and little thick vegetation to hinder the grazing of cattle. The Cherokees were powerful enough to discourage immigration of all but the bravest and hardiest whites into the Spartanburg area until the end of the Cherokee War of 1761. After the defeat of the Indians, settlers from Pennsylvania and all along the Appalachian Mountains poured into the South Carolina piedmont.

Most of the settlers came into the area from the north, and communications with the coast were almost nonexistent. The back country (Spartanburg County was in an area known as Ninety-Six District) was wild, and roaming bands of brigands moved through it, robbing and molesting the population. All legal authority was located in the low country, and the coastal inhabitants showed little concern for the needs, desperate though they may have been, of the back country settlers. Finally, in the late 1760s the back country people took the law into their own hands and formed vigilante bands to rid themselves of the outlaws. The vigilante activity, known as the Regulator Movement, did succeed in getting courts and officers of the law to keep the peace. Not that the area after 1769 was civilized in a coastal sense, but at least there were people to turn to if the law was being grossly violated.

Although the Regulator Movement of the late 1760s focused the attention of the low country on the affairs of the interior parts of the colony, that interest did not outlast the coming of peace. Even though two-thirds of the population of the colony of South Carolina lived in the back country by 1775, the lack of easy land and water travel between the two regions and the difference in their needs and interests acted to separate their existence as if they were two separate colonies. Unless something special happened, people along the coast ignored the nether parts of the colony. Such an occasion was brewing in the 1760s and early seventies when the interests of the low country

13

planters, lawyers, and commercial elements came into conflict with the British authorities. As the colonials and the mother country found themselves increasingly at odds with one another, it became clear to the coastal interests that the support of the back country in the forthcoming struggle would be important.

Back country settlers, having no important and immediate relationship either with the low country or with the British government, were not party to the squabbles so dear to their coastal cousins. Generally, they had little reason to be antagonistic to the British and not much more reason to be favorably disposed to the cause of Charleston. When rumors reached colonial rebels that the back country militia had loyalist leanings (that is loyal to the king), the rebels sent representatives to gain the support of the militia for the rebel cause. The trip of William Henry Drayton and William Tennant on behalf of the rebels to the up country in 1775 proved the extent of the loyalist feeling in the Ninety-Six District. Only in the area of Lawson's Fork, around present-day Spartanburg, did Drayton and Tennant find significant support. Colonel John Thomas of Lawson's Fork raised a militia company, called the Spartan Regiment, to counter the loyalism of the other militia groups in the area. Tradition has it that the county derived its name from this military band. Why the militia chose it is anybody's guess.

The ensuing struggle between loyalist and rebel militia groups in the district during 1775 amounted to a civil war. The key issue turned out to be which group could best ensure the safety and peace of the inhabitants. As it turned out, the loyalists could not do so, and they were ultimately driven underground and dispersed. But the American Revolution would not ignore the back country. In 1779 the British decided to concentrate their efforts on the South, where rebel military leadership had been relatively unsuccessful. Regular British troops were sent into the area to ferret out rebel militia, to establish control over the colony, and to demonstrate the ability of the British army to keep the peace. In a series of battles in Spartanburg District (Cedar Springs, Wofford's Iron Works near modern Glendale, and Musgrove Mill) the rebel militia mauled the British regulars and loyalist recruits.

The British general for the Southern theater, Lord Cornwallis, developed a strategy for moving from South Carolina through North Carolina to crush Washington's army in Virginia. He ordered Colonel Patrick Ferguson to cover his western flank. Ferguson was a fine soldier who had succeeded in rallying support for the British in the back country but had failed to quell the activities of the rebel militia. Ferguson publicly announced his contempt for the rebels, and they in turn determined to destroy him. As Ferguson moved toward King's Mountain in North Carolina to protect Cornwallis, the rebels pursued him. Contrary to his orders, Ferguson decided to make a stand on the mountain and destroy the militia. In the ensuing battle the rebels killed Ferguson and most of his force, thereby making

Jammie Seay fought in the Revolutionary War as a rebel. He owned about five hundred acres around Crescent Avenue, where he built this house in the 1770s. A modest home for a substantial landowner, the house was far more typical of the structures most people of substance lived in during the eighteenth century than were the more elegant homes represented on these pages. People who owned much less acreage lived in even more modest houses of one or maybe two rooms. Seay died in 1850 at the age of ninety-three and was buried in the churchyard cemetery of Saint Timothy's Chapel near Arkwright. The Seay house is the oldest in the city of Spartanburg, and it is currently under restoration.
Photograph by B & B Studio.

A fine example of the type of house occupied by most people in the county in the eighteenth and nineteenth centuries is the Jacob Reynard Frey House in Wellford. The structure was built about 1775 and is important because it shows two features of early buildings in the county: foundations made from large stones and walls chinked with mud to keep out the cold in the winter and the heat in the summer. Many of the still-standing old houses which have clapboards or other covering over them added such sheathing to provide a more sophisticated air when the occupants grew successful enough to worry about such things. The basic structure of most homes from the eighteenth century is heavy timber and dried mud.
Photograph by James Buchanan; courtesy of the Spartanburg County Historical Association.

Cornwallis temporarily give up his plan.

In 1781 Cornwallis tried again and gave orders to the most hated and feared of the British cavalry leaders, Colonel Barnastre Tarleton, to destroy the rebel forces in the back country. This order pitted Tarleton against Colonel Daniel Morgan of the regular American army. On January 16, 1781, realizing that Tarleton was on his heels and that he could not escape, Morgan took his men to Hannah's Cowpens, named for the man who had grazed his cattle there. Because, like other regular army officers, he thought militia unreliable, Morgan placed them on the top of a gentle sloping hill about five miles away from the swollen Broad River, an action which prevented any escape for the rebel troops. As Tarleton later admitted, the disposition of Morgan's troops and the lay of the land were all in the British officer's favor. Due to a mix-up in orders during the battle, part of Morgan's troops retreated when they were supposed to charge. The British troops gleefully pursued, but Morgan's quick recovery in ordering a turnabout left the British troops facing a wall, only ten feet away, of firing troops. The British fled the field, and the rebels won a complete victory. Cowpens was the last battle in the back country, and it thwarted the plans of Cornwallis, whose movement to Virginia ended at Yorktown. Although American generals had contempt for the militia, it proved its worth in the South Carolina piedmont.

Before and after the Revolution, life in the back country was harsh. Most people lived in lean-tos or one-room cabins; some lived in a two-room house divided by a hallway or a single fireplace. They eeked out an existence by growing corn and a few other vegetables and by keeping hogs. Eighteenth century settlers grazed cattle on the bottomlands, but during the nineteenth century those lands were converted to the growing of crops. The good land seems to have been shared by both the small and large landowners. Farming, which was the occupation of over ninety percent of the population, required working from sunup to sunset. Most slaveowners worked in the fields with their slaves, for most people who owned slaves owned only a few. Until the 1840s the large majority of farmers did not grow enough to be able to sell much. Most people lived on the edge of subsistence. Although there were small settlements of a few families scattered in the county, there was only one village, Spartanburg, founded in 1831.

In 1789 settlers had decided to locate a jail and courthouse near a spring on Williamson's plantation. They placed these public buildings facing each other at either end of a large rectangular plot of open land around which lots were laid out. Thus they formed a nucleus which drew business people of various kinds to settle near the public buildings. Today, this area is known as Morgan Square (in 1881 the statue of Daniel Morgan was placed at the west end of the open space where the first courthouse had stood). The spring—the public water supply for man and beast—was located on the north side of the

square between Church and Magnolia streets. Although during the early nineteenth century the village brought together lawyers, merchants, and artisans, life in the county remained rural.

There were some families in the eighteenth, and more in the early nineteenth centuries who had already built substantial homes in the county. The two Moore houses, Walnut Grove and Fredonia, the Price house, and several others, especially the small but elegant Camp Hill, lent an air of elegance and sophistication to the county. The rich and powerful demonstrated such by their fine manor houses and their entertainments. Yet, we must not forget that in most instances those homes look far prettier and better kept now than they did when they were new. Not only were the trees surrounding them much smaller, and the condition of them not nearly as pristine as it is now, but they were working farms. There were pigs and cows around and perhaps a horse or two; slaves and white laborers, working either for wages or for a share, were ever-present. The roads were mud in the rain and dust in the sun; the air smelled of sweat, manure, and other odors of farm life; the wives of the owners spent much of their time tending gardens to feed the family; most women made their own clothes; men made their own furniture and tools. Life was constant work. That world is now, in some sense, lost to us, and we can hardly imagine what life was like for the people who lived in those fine houses we see today.

In the two decades before 1860 Spartanburg did not escape the apprehension which filled the hearts of Southerners at the attack on slavery being waged by other Americans. In 1822 a supposed rebellion had been discovered in Charleston, and subsequent slave insurrections in Haiti had frightened Southern slaveowners as to the reliability of their own slave population. In the 1830s two events occurred which sealed the attitudes of white Southerners toward their human property. One was nullification and the other was Nat Turner's rebellion.

In the late 1820s a tariff had passed the Congress which served to protect infant manufacturing in New England at the expense of Southern cotton growers. The main fear in the South was not so much that imported manufactured goods would now cost much more, as indeed they would, but that if the European countries decided to retaliate, they were bound to lay heavy import duties on Southern cotton. Thus the staple would be less competitive on the world market. By 1832 South Carolina was in the throes of nullification, John C. Calhoun's doctrine that a state had the right to nullify a federal law (in this case the tariff) which that state felt was detrimental to its

On some 450 acres given him by his father, Charles, General Thomas Moore built Fredonia a few miles west of Walnut Grove. A traveler described it as "a hospitable plantation and home," for General Moore's life was "in a backwards state, but on a more refined scale than that presented by the generality of settlers, his circumstances being more independent" (quoted in Writers' Program, Works Projects Administration, A History of Spartanburg County, Spartanburg, S.C., 1940, 46). This photograph was taken in the 1890s and shows the house much as it must have looked in the eighteenth century before the multiple embellishments of later years. The house burned in the 1970s.
Courtesy of the Spartanburg County Historical Association.

Smith's Tavern was built about 1795 and was restored in the mid-1970s. The tapestry chimney is one of the few remaining in the county since an itinerant Dutch mason came through the county in the mid-1770s and hired himself out to build them.
Photograph by Robin Smith; courtesy of the Spartanburg County Historical Association.

The first county justices received their commissions in 1785. It took two years of quarreling before they finally settled on a site for the public buildings of the county. In 1787 they purchased a two-acre tract for five shillings from Thomas Williamson and contracted for the building of a gaol (jail), pillory, whipping post, stocks, and courthouse. The forbidding nature of the first public expenditures by the county accurately reflects the life of this frontier region. The courthouse, constructed of hewn timbers about 1789, contained a courtroom and two jury rooms and was twenty by thirty feet. It was located by the spring in what is presently Morgan Square about where West Main Street and Magnolia intersect.
Photograph courtesy of the Spartanburg Herald-Journal.

interests. In the midst of this acrimonious debate, Spartanburg County residents disagreed with Calhoun and took a pro-unionist stand. Leaders of the unionist forces in the county argued that it was not constitutional for a state to nullify a federal law and that remedies short of such drastic action were possible.

Although Spartanburg remained unionist during the nullification controversy, it had become secessionist by 1850. This drastic change came about largely because of the controversy over slavery. In 1832 the Nat Turner rebellion in Virginia, in which marauding slaves killed several white families, frightened unionists into becoming secessionists. Throughout the South, whites, both slaveowners and non-slaveowners, became frightened of the potential for violence in their midst. In addition, throughout the 1840s and 1850s the activities of the abolitionists in the North seemed intent on provoking that violence. In general, Northerners, although they did not wish to do away with slavery immediately, were becoming amenable to restricting its existence to the Southern states. Southerners, who had once looked upon slavery as a necessary evil, now saw slavery as the cornerstone of all that was good in their society, and they reacted with great emotion to all anti-slavery talk because they saw it as an attack on their superior way of life. During these years residents of Spartanburg County saw things no differently. Even the leaders of unionism in 1832 were, by mid-century, calling for secession from the United States.

During the 1840s and 1850s Spartanburg County took on the trappings of civilization. In 1845 the Limestone Springs Female High School was founded; in 1849 the Reverend Newton Pinckney Walker opened a school for deaf children at Cedar Springs; in 1854 the doors of Wofford College as well as those of Spartanburg Female Academy opened under the auspices of the Methodist Church, and in 1857 schools for boys and girls opened at Reidville. All of the schools not only established reputations for academic work, but also provided local residents with entertainment. The graduation exercises of all the institutions were social occasions for surrounding farmers and residents of the village. People brought picnic lunches, watched the processions, listened to the long speeches, and visited with neighbors and friends. Even people who had no intention or aspiration of sending their children to such places looked on the annual or semi-annual commencements with anticipation and delight.

Outside of these events there was not much entertainment available for people in the mid-nineteenth century. The local churches held socials, there were camp meetings, and people went to

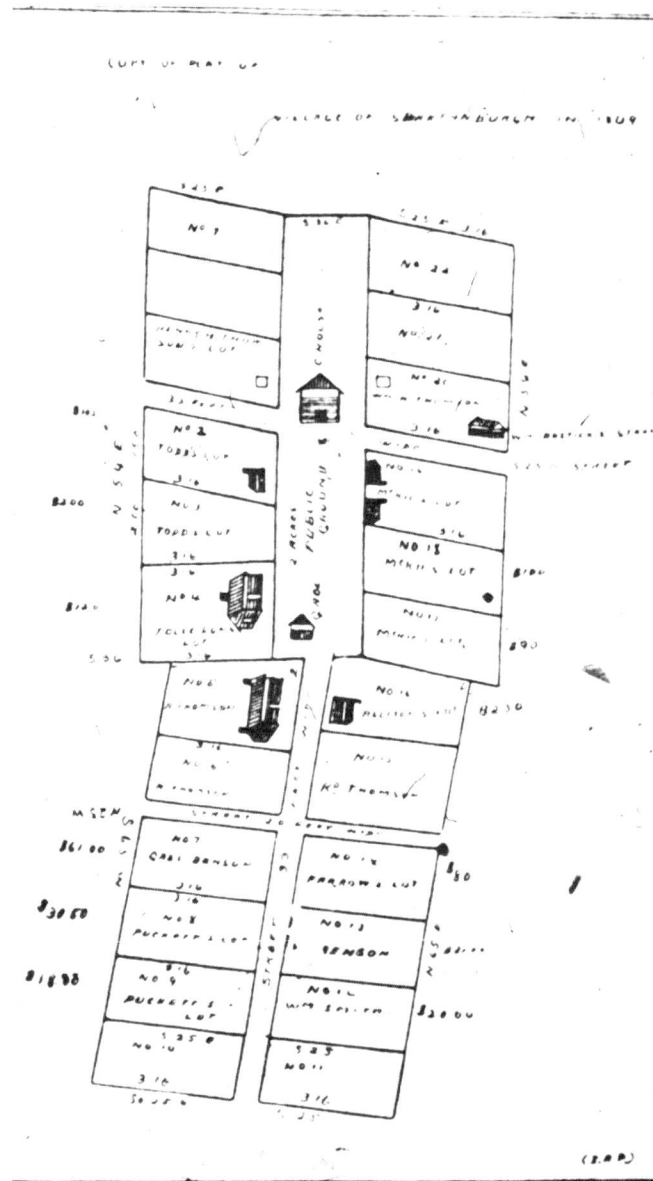

The founder of one of the eminent clans of Spartanburg, Jesse Cleveland came to the county in 1810 and set up storekeeping directly behind the present Cleveland Hotel. He was a keen merchandiser who early realized that he could buy goods more cheaply by making the long trek to Baltimore or Philadelphia himself rather than by trying to get goods in Charleston. He would set out with wagons, slaves, and a parcel of dogs; on his return the dogs would precede him to the village, thus informing everyone that Cleveland would soon be there with new goods to sell. In 1825 he received a land grant of 578 acres, which he increased over the years; he owned much land in the area of the village, especially from Main Street north past Wofford College. Jesse Cleveland was one of the early founders of education for the youngsters of the community, thus inaugurating a tradition of philanthropy in his family which would benefit the village greatly in the future.

Photograph courtesy of Jesse Franklin Cleveland.

the village every Monday for sales day. People from all over the county and some from the mountains brought their goods to sell, and the horses and wagons would fill the village square. For those residents of the county and other parts of the state who could afford the time and money, Spartanburg County offered a number of springs at which people could board for a time and enjoy "the waters" and the leisure. Most famous was Glenn Springs, which was located southeast of Spartanburg village. In addition to the large hotel run by John C. Zimmerman, Glenn Springs had several other homes that opened up to summer visitors. Glenn Springs was located in the heart of a particularly fertile and successful farming region, and its paths and byways were beautiful to stroll and ride along.

By the end of the decade of the 1850s, Spartanburg County had become a substantial rural community. There were a few farmers who had one hundred or more slaves (John C. Zimmerman was the largest slaveowner) and grew cotton in large quantities, and there were some industries. The textile industry got its start before the Civil War with mills in Bivingsville (modern Glendale), Crawfordsville (modern Fairmont), Fingerville, and two very small operations—Valley Falls and Hills. In addition, the county could boast a substantial iron industry with foundries located primarily in the north central and northeastern parts of the county. Most of these were in present day Cherokee County just southwest of the city of Gaffney. During the Civil War both of these industries produced goods for the Confederacy.

Even though there were no military engagements in Spartanburg, the war was a traumatic time for the people who lived there. With sons and husbands away, many never to come home, the county lived on the verge of severe want throughout the war. The years that followed were marked by the strife between rival political factions, the resentment at efforts to bring blacks into the political process, the fraud and corruption which accompanied many of those efforts, and finally the violence of Ku Klux Klan activity in the county. In spite of all the trouble which marked the 1870s, the population of the county tripled, and the economy of the village boomed. In spite of the deprivation of the war years, somehow, somewhere, people got money and they spent it. People craved the goods the war had made them do without. Stories abound of merchants making trips north after the war to buy goods and selling out in only a few days or weeks after returning. There were some fortunes made in the village in those post-war years.

19

Elisha Bomar built this house in 1823 at the corner of Magnolia and Elm (now Saint John) streets, where the courthouse now stands.

Courtesy of the Horace L. Bomar family.

Beautifully sited on the top of a hill, Shiloh Church was built sometime between 1825 and 1830. It is the oldest church building in the county. Tradition has it that Bishop Francis Asbury, the well-known itinerant Methodist preacher, held meetings nearby. Whether the good bishop ever preached here or not, records show that many camp meetings were held on this spot. Located on the Old Blackstock Road (an older Indian trail) linking settlements on the Tyger River with Tryon, North Carolina, the church's location made it a natural gathering place for the Methodists of the area. Religion played an important role in the lives of the frontier people, and their simple and strong faith is reflected in the simplicity which marks the construction of this church. Unadorned, either inside or out, the building has not been altered with time. The original candleholders still line the walls; the benches and stone foundation attest to a primitive craftsmanship. Since 1915 a service has been held here every year, usually on the third Sunday in May.

Photograph courtesy of B & B Studio.

Located at one of the major crossroads in the eastern part of the county, Foster's Tavern served as a "public house" from the time it was built in 1807. The tavern was a popular resting place for travelers going to Glenn Springs from the upper part of the county and is frequently singled out in letters of the antebellum period for its hospitality. In the fashion of the day, columns were added in 1845 and piazzas in 1915. The house stands at the intersections of SC-56 and SC-295. Photograph by James Buchanan; courtesy of the Spartanburg County Historical Association.

Presbyterians organized what is now the oldest congregation in the county in 1765. They built the present structure, known as Nazareth Church, in 1832.

Photograph by James Buchanan; courtesy of the Aug. W. Smith Company.

One of the first schools in the county, this building is a typical one-room schoolhouse. Its location and origins are obscure.

Photograph by James Buchanan; courtesy of the Aug. W. Smith Company.

Central United Methodist Church is the oldest church in the city of Spartanburg. Built in 1837, the church has undergone multiple renovations, the largest of which took place in 1885. The church has always occupied this site on North Church Street.

Photograph courtesy of Wofford College.

This rural slave cabin located behind Camp Hill near Glenn Springs is typical of dwellings for slaves in that it is one room constructed of mud-chinked logs.
Photograph by Linda Taylor Hudgins.

Built in 1834 by Dr. John Winsmith, this small but elegant house is fronted by the original boxwood garden and has an original slave cabin in the back. The house belonged to one of the most colorful politicians in Spartanburg. Dr. Winsmith (who had his name changed by the legislature from Winn Smith) and his brother, Elihu Penquite Smith, were leaders of one of the two most powerful pre-Civil War political factions in the county. Dr. Winsmith challenged the head of the rival faction, James E. Henry, to a duel in 1822, a challenge which Henry treated with contempt.

Winsmith, one of the largest slaveholders in the county and a fire-eating leader for secession, did everything in his life with vigor and bravado. After the war he became a leader of the local Republicans. This shift in loyalties made him the target of much hatred, and not surprisingly he was visited and threatened one night in 1871 by the Ku Klux Klan. Sixty-eight years old at the time, he walked out onto his front porch to face his tormentors with two pistols blazing in his hands and was shot several times. But he was too ornery to die and went on to testify before a Congressional committee against the Klan in the county.
Photograph by Linda Taylor Hudgins.

The Walker House (later known as the Piedmont House) built much of its early business on the reputation for cool and pleasant summers in the upcountry. Although low country people preferred the springs located outside the village, many lodged at the Walker House because of its more pleasant accommodations. Built in the 1840s, the Walker House did not have the high-class reputation of the Palmetto House, but it did provide a favorite watering hole for local and visiting patrons. Town records reveal several instances when the proprietors of the Walker paid fines for selling spirituous liquors when the village was in one of its dry moods. The Walker House, which stood on East Main Street about where the Franklin Hotel is presently located, burned in 1882.

Photograph in the Willis Collection; courtesy of Converse College.

Two Baptist ministers, the Reverend Thomas Curtis and his son, bought the Limestone Springs Hotel in 1845 and converted it into a boarding school for girls. As one of the earliest such schools in the area, it attracted a select and numerous clientele. Instruction was said to be superior; the school opened with a faculty of seven, an unusually high number for its day. In addition to the traditional curriculum, the school offered special lessons in music, drawing, painting, and French. The reputation of the school spread about the state quickly, and by the 1850s girls from all over the two Carolinas were in attendance. The young ladies in this drawing exude just the right air of refinement on which the school prided itself.

Courtesy of the
South Caroliniana Library.

Revolutionary War soldiers discovered that if they bathed in a certain spring located on the Means Plantation they were cured of the "itch." Since such problems were common to frontier living, the spring became quite popular. In 1816 Means sold the spring and surrounding lands to John B. Glenn, who intended to build a house to board summer visitors. In 1845 what had become known as Glenn Springs was purchased by John Conrad Zimmerman, under whose keen guidance the hotel was built, and the area became one of the most popular vacation spots in South Carolina. Even at this early date the water was bottled and sent to eager customers all over the Southeast. The hotel burned in 1941. This photograph dates from the 1880s.

Courtesy of the South Caroliniana Library.

In the last two decades of the antebellum period one-third of the population of the county was slave. Many of these blacks lived in the village, usually quartered in buildings with access from the yard but not from the street. Unlike similar quarters in larger cities such as Charleston, they were not surrounded with high brick walls, but short of that, all was done to discourage unsupervised fraternization among slaves. These quarters are somewhat unusual in that they are brick and built like a motel. Normally, slave quarters were either very large rooms accommodating a number of people or they were individual cabins. The quarters in this photograph were located across East Main Street from the Aug. W. Smith Company.

Photograph by James Buchanan; courtesy of the Spartanburg County Historical Association.

Built in 1850, on the corner of Spring and West Henry streets, this house sat upon a full basement (a "summer kitchen"), as do many Charleston houses. Its owner, J. E. Bomar, was editor of the Carolina Spartan in the mid-1850s and turned to the practice of law in partnership with Colonel John H. Evins after the Civil War. At one time, this house was also used as a hospital by a Dr. Potts. The story is told that Dr. Potts bragged that his patients never suffered from post-operative gas or fever. The first was found to be true because patients were tightly bound about the abdomen with tape, and the latter because the hospital did not possess a thermometer. No wonder some patients feared the hospital more than the disease. The house was demolished in the 1970s.

Photograph by James Buchanan; courtesy of the Spartanburg County Historical Association.

John Conrad Zimmerman built this Greek revival-style house in 1854 in Glenn Springs. It was a fitting house for the successful farmer and owner of the famed hotel. Zimmerman owned thousands of acres of the richest farm land in the county, and his fortune permitted him to help underwrite some of the most successful textile manufacturing ventures in the county.
Photograph by James Buchanan; courtesy of the Aug. W. Smith Company.

After Benjamin Wofford's bequest to found a college was announced, some people within the Methodist church began to agitate for a similar institution for girls, and citizens of the village approached the Methodist officials to place the campus in Spartanburg. Because opposition to placing the college in the village developed within the Methodist conference, local citizens subscribed to purchase land on College Street in what is now Spartan village and built the school in 1854. Things did not go well at the school until W. K. Blake, a North Carolinian, became its president in the late 1850s. Blake took the train to the coast to accompany girls to the school, and during the Civil War managed through his connections and diligence in searching out food to keep the school open until 1863. Low country girls sought refuge from the threatening Yankee armies by spending their school years in Spartanburg. In the 1870s the school became Columbia College and moved to the city of Columbia. By the turn of the century this building became the Good Samaritan Hospital, and in 1914 it was taken over by the United States' Public Health Service to conduct its research into the causes of pellagra. The building was demolished in the 1970s.

Photograph courtesy of William C. Herbert, Jr.

Dr. James Bivings left two imposing houses in the county. The first he built in 1830 at the site of Wofford's Iron Works, where he pioneered in cotton manufacture on a large scale when he erected in the early 1830s a large cotton factory. The area came to be known as Bivingsville, and cotton manufacture continued there without interruption until the mid-twentieth century. Bivings soon lost control of his mill, but he remained undaunted as to the prospects of cotton manufacture in the district, and in the mid-1840s he took over a mill at Crawfordsville. This he successfully operated until he sold it in 1856. In that same year Bivings had completed a beautiful residence in Spartanburg village, setting it on a hill, as he had his house in Bivingsville. This latter home passed into the Evins family and was the residence of John H. Evins, a Congressional representative from Spartanburg in the 1870s and 1880s and an important political figure in the state. Bivings pioneered the concept of the mill village in the upcountry. He set high moral standards for his workers and provided a village for them in order to keep them away from bad influences and under his protection.

Photograph by James Buchanan; courtesy of the Aug. W. Smith Company.

The Reverend Newton Pinckney Walker opened a school for deaf children in 1849 at Cedar Spring. In 1855 the curriculum was expanded to care for the blind, and two years later the state of South Carolina purchased the school and built this fine classical structure. It was always one of the hallmarks of this institution that it kept close ties with the surrounding community. Graduation exercises and other social and academic functions were often open to the public, and the entertainment-starved farmers looked forward to these events.
Photograph by James Buchanan; courtesy of the Spartanburg County Historical Association.

A Spartanburg couple, Judge T. O. P.
Vernon and Harriet Bomar Vernon,
photographed sometime around the
Civil War.

Courtesy of the
Horace L. Bomar family.

The James Lucas House was one of
many beautiful residences built on East
Main Street in the 1870s.
    Photograph by James Buchanan;
        Courtesy of the
        Spartanburg County
        Historical Association.

Looking almost ethereal in the snow, this house stood on the southern corner of Pine and East Main streets. The slate mansard roof, heavy in both actuality and appearance, was one of the very few in the city and stood in marked contrast to most of its neighbors, which were Victorian houses awash in fancy woodwork. The house was built in the 1870s by the Bomar family and was lived in for years by Stanyarne Wilson, a local lawyer and later a congressman. In his early years Wilson built a reputation for defending cotton mill workers against the power of the mill owners, and on the basis of this activity he got himself elected to Congress, where he mellowed very quickly.

Photograph courtesy of the Horace L. Bomar Family.

In his will of 1850 the Reverend Benjamin Wofford left $100,000 for the founding of a college "for literary, classical and scientific education, to be located in my native District of Spartanburg, and to be under the control and management of the Methodist Episcopal Church...." For many years the Main Building (circa 1856) was the entire college, housing a chapel, lecture rooms, laboratories, offices, and a museum. At present the Main Building houses classrooms, offices, a chapel, and an auditorium. The Main Building was designed by Edward C. Jones of Charleston and built with slave labor by Clayton and Burgess of Asheville, North Carolina. Although the exterior of the building was impressive, the materials used in its construction were weak; the·interior of the very thick walls was constructed of soft brick, and during construction the western tower collapsed and killed one man. This mid-1850s daguerreotype is the oldest photograph of Spartanburg County known to the author.

Courtesy of the
University of Georgia Library.

Two of these young men were native Spartans, the future physician Jesse Cleveland in the middle and Barnett Franklin Cleveland on his left. The two Spartans and their unidentified friend were serving in the South Carolina Militia guarding the coast in Charleston sometime in the 1860s when this picture was taken. Jesse seems either to have given up a Napoleonic pose, gotten very warm, or become absent-minded about his appearance.

Photograph courtesy of
Jesse Franklin Cleveland.

The youth of this Confederate soldier represents the pressures and strains placed on the manpower of the South during the Civil War.

Photograph courtesy of
J. H. McMillin.

Although no battles were fought in Spartanburg County, during the latter years of the Civil War the village was full of wounded soldiers. As the last stop on the Spartanburg and Union Railroad, completed in 1859, Spartanburg village was the first destination of soldiers heading home from the battlefields. Citizens outfitted this house on North Converse Street (next to the present location of Saint Paul's Church) as a temporary hospital for the care of those wounded who could not immediately set out for home on foot or wagon. Local women formed a nursing corps and alternated working at the station for days at a time. Many people in the village also took soldiers into their homes, met soldiers at the train station with food and much-needed blankets, and sometimes even took them to out-of-the-way farms in their buggies. The Confederate Aid Station was used later as a hospital by Dr. P. N. Nott, who operated in a room with a slate floor with a drain in the middle. In late nineteenth century surgery, the drain was probably one of the surgeon's most useful tools. Last used as a boarding house, the building is no longer standing.

Photograph courtesy of
William C. Herbert, Jr.

In a style uncharacteristic of the time,
Hattie Gentry let her hair fall to her
waist in this formal portrait taken in
1880. She was sixteen at the time.
Courtesy of Jennie Rhinehart.

1880-1920

In 1880 Spartanburg became a city. The threefold increase in the town's population during the 1870s had prompted town officials to make that request of the state legislature. It may have seemed presumptuous of the leaders of a town of 3,200 population to change their official status from that of village to that of city, but in some ways the next twenty years made them look like seers. In the last two decades of the nineteenth century Spartanburg acquired many of the trappings of the larger cities it emulated. In the early seventies kerosene lamps dotted the square, but gas lamps replaced them in 1882. The beginnings of a firefighting unit organized in 1873 achieved the status of a fire department some nine years later when the city bought its first fire engine. The equipment was the city's, but the firefighters were volunteers. Water, first obtained from the spring and then from a public well in the middle of the square, became available through the Home Water Supply Company in 1888. The company supplied fifty hydrants and four public drinking fountains for man and horse. In the last two decades of the nineteenth century anything calling itself a city had to have paving and some open space to show off the buildings of progress, so the trees lining the square were cut, the old public well was filled in, and the look of the square changed.

In 1889 several citizens, under the leadership of Dexter Converse, established Converse College and thereby took a step that had a profound effect on the cultural life of the county. The college not only provided good education for young ladies, but it also sponsored and hosted musical and theatrical productions which became an important part of the county's intellectual life. With the inauguration of the South Atlantic States Music Festival in 1895, the close relationship between town and gown in entertainment and musical education became fixed.

The beginnings of modernization which took place in the eighties bore fruit in the nineties. The city let contracts for electric street lights and sewage disposal in 1890 and began a program of expensive street renovation. One mile of macadamized street was laid and the sidewalks were cemented. In 1892 that symbol of mass transit, the streetcar, appeared on East Main Street running from the railroad crossing just west of Liberty to Pine Street. It resembled New York City's 1820s horse-drawn car that had inaugurated mass transit in the United States. There was a Southern touch in Spartanburg, however, for its car was drawn by a mule. An engine replaced Spartanburg's mule within a week, but it promptly blew up. All innovation cannot be trouble-free.

The Spartanburg Railway, Gas and Electric Company relaced the pioneer traction company in the early nineties and eventually constructed a city system running from Union Station on Magnolia to Main Street. From there the tracks went east to Church, where they ran both north and south. From the corner of East Main and Church the tracks went up Main to Pine Street, where they connected with a suburban line which ran along Pine to Country Club Road and on to Glendale, Clifton, and Converse. From the corner of Pine and Main streets the city line continued east up Main to Rock Cliff Park on Heywood Avenue. Another line turned westward on Main at Morgan Square and went to Saxon. By 1906 this company had some fifteen miles of track; popular routes on weekends were those to Rock Cliff Park and to Glendale Park, which bordered the Glendale Mill. Spartanburg, city and county, prospered during these years from 1880 to 1920. Downtown Spartanburg city bustled with stores, people, and traffic. The automobile began to appear, and in those first years when cars, horses, trains, and trolleys vied for the right-of-way, pedestrians jeopardized their lives just by being on the streets.

Spartanburg owed much of its prosperity to the railroads. Men with capital were willing to invest in the area because the railroads were here to transport goods. By 1900 rail lines crisscrossed the county to all four points of the compass. From the north to Atlanta and from Asheville to Charleston, Spartanburg was "on the way" to almost everywhere. Local capitalists invested in and used the rails. When Dexter Converse built additional mills he constructed rail lines to connect with the major railways; when the Charleston and Western Carolina line went broke, a Spartanburg man, John B. Cleveland, bought it. Cleveland abandoned the old emphasis on passengers and concentrated on freight, a wise choice which presaged the future and made him some money. The Spartanburg business community had realized early in the 1840s that it was in keen competition for rails, for the cities that got the railroads would prosper. By the late nineteenth century the promoters had been successful and the rails had come: the Charleston and Western Carolina, the Southern, and the Piedmont and Northern.

The county's income and pride were hurt in 1897 when Gaffney, its largest town, and the upper northeastern part of the county split away and joined with parts of York and Union to form Cherokee County. In the long run, the increase in textile activity during the last part of the nineteenth century overshadowed the economic loss of Gaffney. Investors built several mills in the county, and Captain John H. Montgomery, who had first come to the county as a fertilizer salesman, built the first cotton mill in the city of

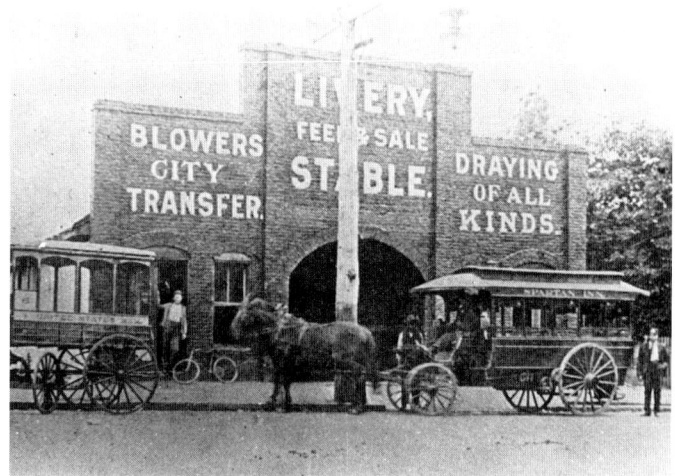

The United States mail service in the 1880s.
Photograph in the Willis collection; courtesy of the Aug. W. Smith Company.

The dining room at the Glenn Springs Hotel looked like this around the turn of the century.

Photograph courtesy of Ned Austell.

Spartanburg. He named it Spartan Mill. Two years later, in 1890, a subscription was launched in the city to start Beaumont Mills; by 1909 there were nine mills in or near the city of Spartanburg.

There was little concentration of population outside of the immediate villages, and textile mills had to provide living quarters for their employees. As early as the 1850s, John Bivings had erected a small village at Crawfordsville to provide living space for his workers. In the latter part of the nineteenth and early twentieth centuries, mill operators did the same. In order to have their workers close to the mill, to provide them with the necessities of life, and to have some control over the type of worker which they employed, mill owners built villages around their plants. The mill owned the houses and rented them to workers; stores owned by the company provided workers with the basic necessities, including credit. This process created some distance between the mill workers and the inhabitants of the city, a phenomenon not so unusual since the two came to live in almost separate worlds.

In spite of the increase in the number of textile mills, the county remained overwhelmingly agricultural. After the Civil War the number of large farms decreased as land was divided among sharecroppers and tenants. With the dismantling of slavery, landowners became convinced that the cost of large-scale farming was prohibitive, so they took on families to whom they rented land. The most common method of farming was sharecropping, under which arrangement the landowner would rent the land either for a portion of the crop grown on it or for cash. The local merchant granted the tenant credit for fertilizer, seed, and other goods against a lien on the future crop. When the harvest came in, the sharecropper or tenant sold it through the local merchant. Since the merchant took a risk that the crop might be small or might fail completely, he usually charged the tenant from twenty to seventy-five percent interest on the loan. Cotton prices were not good, and most tenants were in perpetual debt to landowner and merchant.

In general, farming had two primary enemies before the Civil War. The first was erosion, and the second was partly a consequence of the first—loss of fertility in the soil. Heavy rains and habitual planting without taking precautions to prevent erosion left the rolling hills of the county barren of good topsoil. Farmers in the antebellum South did little to try to restore fertility to the soil, believing either that there was nothing they could do about it or that they could move on. Even when the new land began to run out, local farmers did surprisingly little to restore the growing power of their land. By the 1880s men came South, bringing with them the fertilizers necessary to re-enrich the soil. Because of fertilizers and rising price people grew more cotton in Spartanburg after the Civil War than before it.

Cotton seemed the best and possibly the only cash crop available to them, so the farmers of the county, no matter how small an operation they had, devoted themselves to raising the staple of their ancestors. Fertilizers allowed them to produce much more per acre than ever before. Because of this single-mindedness, they would sometimes profit and oftentimes suffer. When cotton was plentiful and prices went down, farmers refused to limit their production; there was no organization to help them to do it, and every farmer believed he could get a good price by selling his crop before everyone else did. Even when farmers realized what was going on, they had no choice. To grow less while others grew more was folly. There seemed no way out of the dilemma.

In 1917 America declared war. When the United States government announced that it was looking for training centers, several city leaders successfully lobbied on Spartanburg's behalf. By the middle of 1917 the War College scheduled a camp to be placed a little more than three miles west of the city (the camp was located in and around Westgate Mall). The War College named the facility in honor of a New York Civil War volunteer, Brigadier General James S. Wadsworth, partly because a New York division, made up of that state's national guard, was to be trained in Spartanburg. So the 27th Division, a rather bluestocking crowd of "Yankees" commanded by Major General John F. O'Ryan, was to descend on the rural and small (about 22,000) city of Spartanburg. And descend they did. But even before they arrived, it began to dawn on the city and county what this training amounted to. The camp required 915 buildings besides ten storehouses and a hospital unit, all to be built within a few months. The men would sleep in tents. Upwards of forty thousand men who eventually moved through the camp swamped the little town of Spartanburg and taxed it beyond its limits for entertainment and diversion. The almost two years of the camp's existence was a difficult but rewarding time for the county and city.

Between 1885 and 1920 Spartanburg's architecture underwent a change so radical as to leave it a different city. It was as if the spirit of optimism which infused the leaders of the village drove them into an unthinking destruction of the old so they could build all anew. The old village landmarks went one by one, some by hazard and most by design. The square, which was really a rectangle, had assumed its character from a row of interesting buildings on its north side beginning with the Opera House and moving eastward to the Palmetto House. By 1910 all were gone, some replaced with buildings of distinction, others with buildings of mammon. It seemed as if structures on the north side of Daniel Morgan were especially ill-fated; many buildings on the south side remain there still. Unfortunately, those structures were considerably less distinguished. The destruction went on laboriously: the Palmetto House, the Courthouse, the Opera House, the First National Bank, and the Spartan Inn. Some distinguished earlier buildings such as the old jail were not on the square, but even they met destruction during these years.

The city that grew in place carried the stamp of the Victorian era. Although somewhat out of favor in our own day, much of the architecture and building of the turn of the century was a credit: the

Although the fame of the Glenn Springs area as a summer resort had spread as early as the 1840s, the heyday of the region occurred in the latter part of the nineteenth and the early part of the twentieth centuries. This photograph of the hotel, its staff, and its guests dates from the 1880s. Whatever fame was achieved by Spartanburg County during this time was the product of either the infamous activities of the Ku Klux Klan in the

early 1870s or the well-deserved praise showered on the beautiful wooded environs of Glenn Springs.

The routine that hotel guests followed seems blissfully dull in our harrowed age. People used to take the water early in the day, walk along the lovely wooded paths, eat heartily in the well-appointed dining room, take some more water at the spring, and sit and let the hours go by. The hours passed as guests made use of the many rocking chairs provided on the long verandah. Children used to love to play under the hotel (there was not much for children to do), which sat up on posts, for the air was cool and comfortable. In the evenings, people played whist or attended parties and danced just as they had since the 1840s when guests had traveled many miles to Glenn Springs' parties. The railroad built to Glenn Springs in the last part of the nineteenth century made all of this leisure more accessible, and thousands took advantage of it. By the third decade of the twentieth century the resort had diminished in importance, and in 1941 the hotel burned. Today the area is still beautiful, but no one goes there.

Photograph courtesy of the South Caroliniana Library.

41

Glenn Springs got its fame from its spring water, which was bottled in this plant and sent all over the world. The photograph dates from the 1880s.

Photograph courtesy of the South Caroliniana Library.

Cleveland Law Range, the new courthouse, and the many Victorian houses on Pine and Church streets. There were also some classical buildings, such as the city hall and the United States Post Office, which added a new dimension and a change from the Victorian. The two finest additions to the new city were exquisite products of the new age. For Spartanburg they were towering skyscrapers; each, in its heyday, harkened to a skyscraper style which went back to the late nineteenth century, luckily for Spartanburg, for they both reflected an artistry in architecture which in many ways was indigenously American. The Andrews Building (originally called the Chapman Building) was constructed in 1912 and the Montgomery Building in 1923. The architectural details and the wholistic impression of both of these buildings is impressive, even if it can only be appreciated in photographs, for both buildings are gone: the Andrews destroyed in an aborted demolition attempt in 1977 and the Montgomery radically changed into a shell of its former self. Yet such change was part of a wider reconstitution of the city which occurred after World War II, when, in an attempt once again to reflect progress as others saw it, Spartanburg destroyed this second generation of buildings to construct yet a third. These last, unfortunately, reflected an alien presence in American architecture which denied the local and copied the international, a style which was particularly subject to bad imitation. So the post office, the courthouse, the city hall, the Andrews and Montgomery buildings all went the way of their precursors.

Built in 1850 by Junius Thomson at the corner of East Main and North Church streets, the Palmetto House was long one of Spartanburg's leading hotels. Spartanburg society used it for parties, dinners, and meetings, making it the place to be seen and heard until the late 1870s. Touted, at least locally, as one of the finest hotels in the state, it seemed not to lack for out-of-town guests. But all was not gaiety within its walls, for political meetings were frequently held there. In November of 1860 the Palmetto House hosted the meeting which sent county delegates to South Carolina's secession convention. After the late 1870s the Palmetto retained a shadow of its social importance, thanks largely to the presence of the popular Becker's Oyster Saloon and Ice Cream Parlor. This mid-1880s photograph shows the deteriorating condition of the building. Having outlived its glory, the hotel was torn down in the early nineties and replaced with the Palmetto Building, devoted to stores and offices.

Albert H. Twitchell built this house in 1882. Twitchell came south in 1859 to help his brother-in-law, Dexter Converse, run the Bivingsville mill. In 1870 he joined with Converse and others in buying the mill and became the treasurer of the D. E. Converse Company. For many years Twitchell served as organist in the Presbyterian church, and in 1895 he founded the annual Festival of Music which became one of the special cultural events in the area. His interest in education was as keen as in music; he was one of the original subscribers of Converse College. The Twitchell house stood on the corner of Pine and Glendalyn streets.

Photograph by James Buchanan;
courtesy of the
Aug. W. Smith Company.

Victorian building in the 1880s was not confined to Pine Street. Bishop William W. Duncan of the Methodist church built this house on North Church Street just north of Central Methodist Church in 1885. The photograph dates from the turn of the century.

South of Albert H. Twitchell's house on Pine Street, where the county library now stands, Dexter Converse built his residence in 1889. These two fine Victorian houses give some feeling for the elegance that was Pine Street in the late nineteenth century.

Photograph, 1889,
courtesy of Stanley Converse.

It is fitting that two of the most substantial-looking and most elegant mansions built in the city in the 1880s should have been built for the Cleveland brothers. John B. and Dr. Jesse Cleveland were engaged in land speculation and various business ventures in and around Spartanburg. Their names appear on almost all the boards of directors of the new companies being formed in the latter half of the nineteenth century. John B. Cleveland listed himself in the city directory as a "capitalist." Family tradition has it that the two brothers were very fond of each other; each one named his first son for his brother, a fact that has caused countless difficulties for historians trying to keep the family lines straight. In the 1880s the two brothers built identical homes. Dr. Jesse, who stopped practicing medicine to manage his business affairs, built his house on Howard Street where the Cleveland school is presently located, and John B. built his house—named Bonhaven—on the north side of the intersection of North Church Street and the Asheville Highway.

The residence of Jesse Cleveland on Howard Street, 1882.
Photograph courtesy of Jesse Franklin Cleveland.

Henry and Jesse Cleveland stand before Bonhaven, built in 1884 by their father, John B. Cleveland.
Photograph courtesy of Dexter Cleveland.

The big event of the week in the nineteenth century was sales day. Every Monday wagons carrying provisions and goods from the county and from the North Carolina mountains would gather together in Morgan Square. People who had traveled far camped out by the spring behind the courthouse. Not only was this market day for everyone in the area, but it was also an opportunity to exchange gossip, visit with the neighbors, and frequent the local shops and saloons. This earliest picture of Morgan Square shows the Opera House with the tower and clock on the right. Notice the open space under the tower, where ladies could be let off a wagon or buggy to enter the building without getting wet in the rain. Actually a city hall, the building included a hall for theatricals and special events. Next to it stands the Merchant's Hotel, later known as the Spartan Inn, and the building with the columns on the far right is the courthouse. The third courthouse in the county's history, it was built in 1856 entirely of brick, and the columns were coated with white plaster. The monument which gave its name to the square was placed there with great ceremony in the spring of 1881 to mark the one hundredth anniversary of the Battle of Cowpens. Spartanburg was chosen as the place to commemorate the battle because of the inaccessibility of the battleground itself.

Photograph in the Willis Collection; courtesy of the Aug. W. Smith Company.

The first telephone in Spartanburg County ran from this store in the city to Cate's store in Glenn Springs. Photograph, 1888, courtesy of Mrs. W. C. Cannon.

Roman Catholics seem to have moved into Spartanburg County in the middle of the nineteenth century, but not until 1883 were there a sufficient number of Catholics and sufficient funds to build a church of their own. In that year local Catholics built Saint Paul's on North Dean Street. The building was an American Gothic miniature replica of Saint Patrick's in Charleston. The building was extensively renovated in the late 1930s. This photograph dates from about 1900.

Photograph courtesy of Wofford College.

South Carolina has a long tradition of local militia through which Carolinians have shown great pride in the martial spirit. In the antebellum period many such military companies sprang up within the state; some were mostly interested in socializing, but others actually drilled weekly and took the military aspect seriously. One of the best-known of the latter was the Washington Light Infantry from Charleston. In 1856 this company came to Spartanburg to commemorate the Battle of Cowpens. The presence of this fine military encampment on the grounds of Saint John's School, where Converse College now stands, inspired some villagers to form a company of their own; thus, the Morgán Rifles were born. They drilled, paraded, and often held shooting exhibitions where rather elaborate prizes were awarded; as local entertainment such affairs struck the fancy of the population. This 1887 photograph with the snappy uniforms and serious demeanor testifies to the vitality of the organization and the continuing belief among Spartans in a reliance on local militia.

Photograph courtesy of the Spartanburg County Historical Association.

Having received their first uniforms in 1881, the Spartanburg City Police lined up on West Main Street in 1885 for a department photograph. From right to left: Chief J. H. Blassingame, Jim Mullinax, Joe B. Bates, John Sprouse, John Jackson, and Ed Gentry. In 1889 the uniforms would be changed to those familiar across the nation in that day—the uniform reminiscent of the English "bobby." Lionel Lawson remembers hearing the city chain gang sing a ditty when John Floyd was mayor and John Hill chief of police: "Chief Hill gave the orders; Chambers rang the bell; Joe Bates brought 'em in; and John Floyd gave 'em hell." Joe Bates turned out to be a better policeman than husband; in 1910 he shot and killed his wife. Of course, he was retired by that time.

Photograph in the Willis Collection; courtesy of Converse College.

Elisabeth Emily Cleveland reflects the demeanor of the Victorians of the 1880s, a time when people believed that more was wonderful. Thus, the heavy clothes and overstuffed chair.
Photograph courtesy of Jesse Franklin Cleveland.

In the newest fashion of the 1880s, Hattie Gentry celebrates her wedding day in an ankle-length dress with a long, trailing veil.
Photograph courtesy of Jennie Rhinehart.

Under the leadership of Dexter Converse several Spartanburg businessmen subscribed funds to found Converse College in the late 1880s. While the Main Building was under construction these same men founded a private school to prepare the girls for the rigors of college work. Mattie B. Gamewell, who had been teaching in the public schools, accepted the position of teacher in the Converse Fitting School, and Dexter Converse provided a small house on Kennedy Street (directly behind the Piedmont Club) for the school. Miss Gamewell is seen here with her first class of students in 1889.
Photograph courtesy of Converse College.

50

Mary Seay and her sister, Sally, were direct descendants of the Revolutionary War soldier Jammie Seay, whose house is the oldest in Spartanburg. The Seay sisters always referred to themselves as "us gals." Throughout their lives they wore homespun and never went without a bonnet. All their furniture, as well as everything else in their house, was made at home. Ann Sanders Fraser remembers visiting the Seay sisters in the early nineties—always considered a treat by the children—and taking them some gelatin. "Us gals" would not eat the gelatin, however, for when they saw it shake they were convinced that it was alive. The photograph, believed to show Mary Seay, probably dates from the 1890s.

Photograph courtesy of Ann Sanders Fraser.

51

John A. Henneman stands before his jewelry store on Morgan Square in the 1880s. Henneman came to Spartanburg in 1859 and served as mayor in the late 1880s. He proved himself feisty when he braved the anger of a mob and spiked a cannon they had wheeled before the city jail in an effort to remove and hang a prisoner accused of a heinous crime. By driving a spike into the hole at the top of the cannon, out of which protruded the fuse, and by breaking off the spike with a side blow of the hammer, making it impossible to remove the spike, Henneman rendered the cannon useless.

On September 27, 1891, Henneman heard a black couple quarreling in a house and went in to quiet them. Henneman and the black man came out of the house shouting at each other. When the black man went back inside Henneman said, "You are going after your pistol, are you?" and drew his own and also went into the house. A shot was heard, and the two men came rolling out of the door. The black man had Henneman's gun and he shot him with it. John Henneman died a few minutes later.

Built on Magnolia Street across from the court house in the late 1880s, the Cleveland Building housed law offices and the headquarters of the various business interests of John B. and Jesse Cleveland. The building, commonly called the Cleveland "Law Range," has recently undergone restoration. This photograph dates from the 1950s.
Photograph by B & B Studio.

In 1889 the city of Spartanburg built its first public school on Magnolia Street on the north side of the courthouse. Today the courthouse occupies the entire block.
Photograph from the Willis Collection; courtesy of the Aug. W. Smith Company.

52

The Pacolet Cotton Mill was developed through the cooperation over the years of Captain John H. Montgomery and Seth Milliken. In 1881 the firm of Walker, Fleming and Company, under the advice of one of its members, Captain Montgomery, purchased the site for the Pacolet Mill. Walker, Fleming and Company invested heavily in many enterprises in Spartanburg County during the last half of the nineteenth century. Although no mills or other businesses in which they had stock carried their name, this Spartanburg firm was responsible for the major portion of the capitalization of many of the well-known businesses in the county. All of the goods produced by Pacolet Mills were sold through the Deering-Milliken Company of New York. Thus began an association between Southern and Northern capital interests which would prove crucial to the financial well-being of the county.

A bird's-eye view of the city of Spartanburg in 1891.
Courtesy of the Spartanburg Herald-Journal.

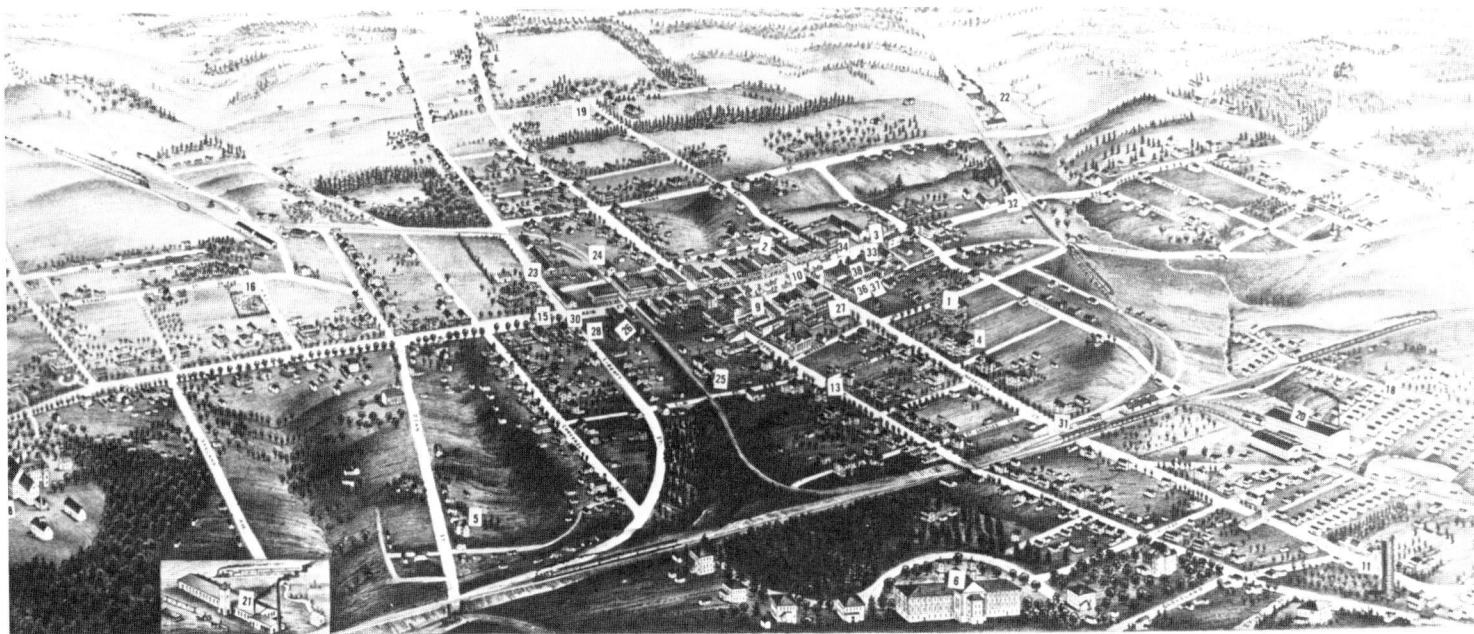

BIRD'S-EYE VIEW OF THE CITY OF
SPARTANBURG,
LOOKING SOUTH EAST.
POPULATION IN 1880, 3200. SOUTH CAROLINA. POPULATION IN 1890, 6000.
1891.

The lobby and office of the Spartan Inn in the 1890s.

Photograph courtesy of Wofford College.

The Merchant's Hotel, later known as the Spartan Inn, was built in 1880. The street floor was given over to shops and some of the rooms on the upper floors were rented as offices but most of the upper rooms were used by the hotel. Standing on Morgan Square between the Opera House and the old courthouse, the Spartan Inn was for thirty years the most photographed building in the city. This photograph was probably made in the early 1890s, for the trees which stood in front of the Inn in the picture of the square taken in 1883 are now gone. The hotel had a special carriage, here parked in front of the entrance to the lobby, to carry patrons to and from the railway stations. The "Whitman's" sign belongs to C. D. Whitman, who styled himself Spartanburg's "iron king" in his ads for iron stoves and other hardware.

Photograph in the Willis Collection; courtesy of the Spartanburg Herald-Journal.

This iron fountain used to stand on the east end of Morgan Square. The picture was taken before 1892 on what was obviously a cold if not snowy day. From the journals, letters, and newspapers of the latter half of the nineteenth century it appears that cold weather was more prevalent than it is today. The fountain now stands on the Converse campus. In 1892 the city council had ordered the fountain removed from the square, and Coverse asked the city to give it to the college. The council refused and ordered it sold at auction; Converse College was the highest bidder.

Photograph courtesy of
B & B Studio.

At about midnight on January 2, 1892, a cry went up in the Main Building at Converse College that the kitchen was on fire. The girls lined up with pitchers in hand to try to quell the blaze. Volunteer firemen from Spartanburg arrived on this bitterly cold night to find that their hoses were too short to reach the college from the nearest fire hydrant. When the hoses from all three volunteer firefighting groups were linked, they barely reached the building. Then the final disappointment: the water pressure was only sufficient to throw water ten feet into the air. In dismay the men rushed to the annex and hosed it down so the fire would not spread; meanwhile, they watch helplessly as the Main Building was engulfed in the flames. Many citizens rushed through the building as the flames spread, saving all they could, but most of the college's equipment, books, and the personal belongings of the students were lost. This photograph, taken the morning after the fire, shows how little remained. Thankfully, the spirit that had founded the college saw it through: classes were resumed, the girls were boarded, and a subscription was begun to build a new building.

Photograph courtesy of
Converse College.

After a bitter fight over the destruction of the old courthouse shown in the 1884 picture of Morgan Square, the fourth courthouse in the county's history was built in 1891. It stood on Magnolia Street on the same site as the present courthouse. The bell and clock in the tower were once in the Opera House on the square and now are housed in the special tower erected in the Main Street Mall. The fourth courthouse, shown here as it looked at mid-century, was destroyed in 1959.
Photograph courtesy of B & B Studio.

Family reunions have long played an important role in the social life of the county. In the mid-1890s the Snoddy and Benson families held one of their annual reunions at the Snoddy residence in Wellford. The house still stands on Highway 29 at the intersection with I-85.
Photograph courtesy of Rosa Black.

John B. Cleveland was born in 1848 in Spartanburg. He graduated from Wofford College in 1869 and trained as a lawyer. His major success, however, was in business, where he amassed a fortune in land, textiles, and railroads. He was for many years the president of the Whitney Manufacturing Company and the Charleston and Western Carolina Railway. By the turn of the century, John B. Cleveland was Spartanburg's foremost citizen, and the city as well as private organizations such as Wofford and Converse colleges were the beneficiaries of his generosity. He died in 1928.

Photograph courtesy of
Wofford College.

The five Benson sisters gathered for a separate portrait which, with a single exception, they seemed to take very seriously.

Photograph courtesy of
Rosa Black.

Cedar Grove, built about 1825, is one of the oldest houses in Glenn Springs and is currently under restoration. Known by some as the Maurice Moore House, by others as the Chapman House, but by most as Cedar Grove, this structure was moved from Cedar Grove to Glenn Springs. This photograph was taken in the late nineteenth century.

Courtesy of
Russell Stevenson.

This photograph of the railroad station on the Southern line at Wellford was taken in the early 1890s. The man to the left of the post is Dr. Hugh R. Black, who was destined to become Spartanburg's leading physician and founder of the Mary Black Hospital.

Photograph courtesy of
Rosa Black.

Like most residents of Glenn Springs, the Chapmans took in boarders in the summer. This picture, taken in the early 1890s, shows the Chapman children with their boarders of that season. Second from the left in the second row is Florence Chapman; her brother Jeff and her sister Rosa stand second and third from the left in the back row. The girl in the window, so coquettishly hiding most of her face, was Susan, who, although too shy to stand with the others, consented to peek out of the window. Although the Glenn Springs Hotel accommodated the largest number of summer guests, so many people wanted to summer here that private houses rented out rooms.

Photograph courtesy of
Russell Stevenson.

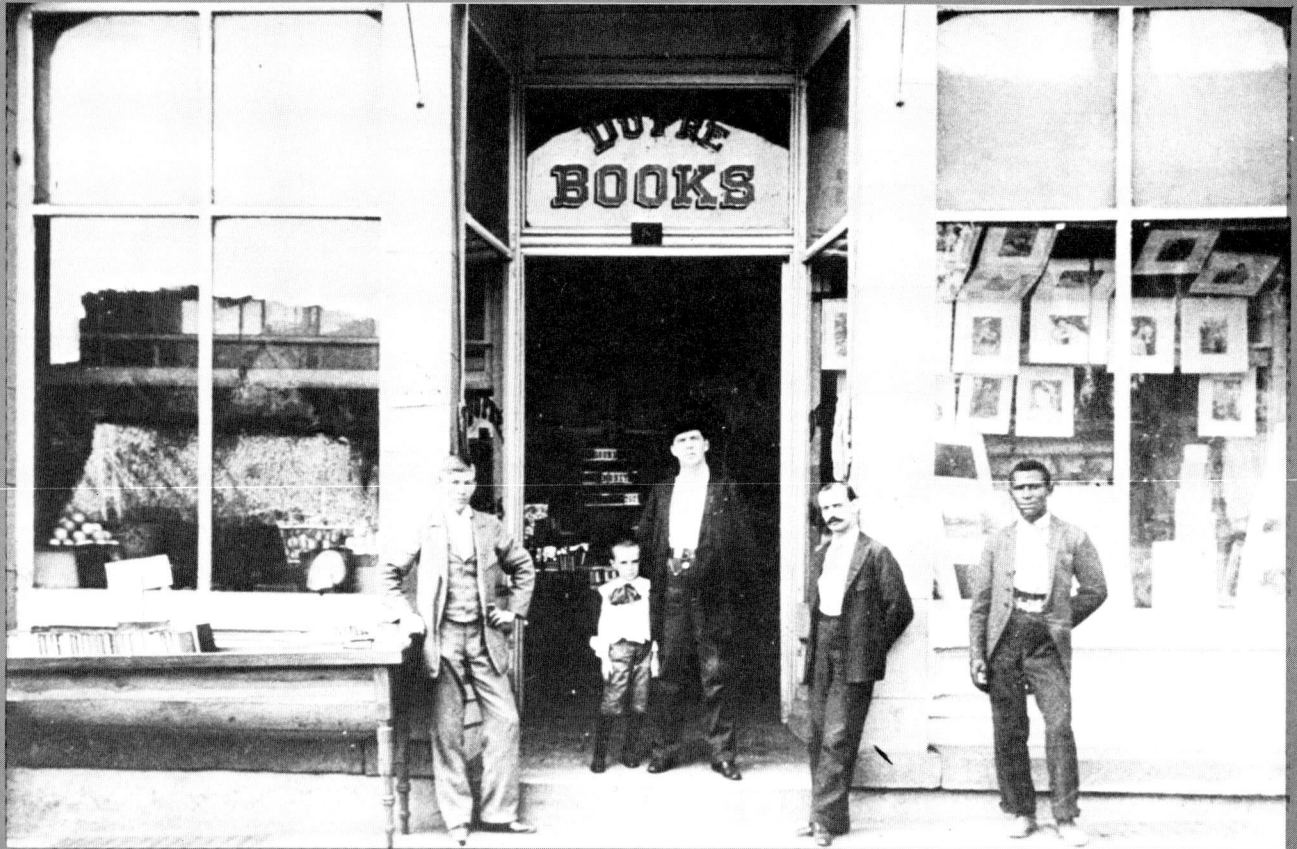

Dupre's Book Store was founded in 1852 and was long a part of the intellectual life of the county. In this mid-nineties photograph the store is on Morgan Square; it later moved to East Main Street. Dupre's offered new and used books, stationery, prints, pens and other office supplies. It was also a place where people gathered to gossip, look leisurely through books, and generally to wile away the hours. Warren Dupre, who assumed control in 1887, stands in the doorway with his son Wallace; to his right is Gabriel Cannon and to his left is a clerk, Samuel L. Cavis, and a porter whose name is unknown.

Photograph courtesy of Mrs. W. C. Cannon.

The T. C. Duncan Syndicate, made up of prominent Spartanburg businessmen, made themselves very unpopular among "history buffs" in the latter quarter of the nineteenth century. The syndicate purchased the Palmetto House on the corner of North Church and East Main streets and replaced it with a block of stores. In 1891 the same group bought the old courthouse and replaced it with this building which, when this picture was taken in 1895, housed Greenewald's and law offices. Many citizens did not consider either change to be for the better.

Photograph courtesy of the Spartanburg Herald-Journal.

In 1897 the Converse yearbook, Y's and OTHER Y's, included a picture of the custodial staff. The caption of that day—"Our Servants"—says a great deal about that era.

Photograph courtesy of Converse College.

OUR SERVANTS

A Spartanburg farmer stacks his corn at the turn of the century. Corn was the major part of a farm family's diet throughout the nineteenth century; if the season was good and the farmer had enough to sell, the corn crop could provide a substantial portion of a farmer's income.

Photograph courtesy of Jennie Rhinehart.

Sometime in the last years of the nineteenth century John Weste Harris lined up his family for a portrait. The children appear bemused, the mule stoic, and Mrs. Harris (the former Hattie Gentry) seems content with her seven children. Typical of farm families of the time, there were two more children to come. Also typical is the small farm house to accommodate this brood. From left to right the children are: Carlos, John, Hattie, Julia, Gentry, Lyles, and Emily.

Photograph courtesy of Jennie Rhinehart.

These young women made up the first
graduating class from Converse College
when they sat for their portrait in 1897;
they were outnumbered by Wofford's
class of that same year, perhaps
agreeably so far as the girls were
concerned.

These formal children's portraits were all taken in the middle 1890s.

Mary and Mildred Patterson
Photograph courtesy of
Dexter Cleveland.

Sam Orr Black, Sr., sat in his wagon for this photograph taken with an unidentified playmate.
Photograph courtesy of
Rosa Black.

Donald and David Sanders.
Photograph courtesy of
Ann Sanders Fraser.

Dexter Edgar Converse was born in Vermont in 1829 and came south to run the Bivingsville Mill for John Bomar in the 1850s. In the mid-1870s Converse bought the mill and renamed the community in which it was located Glendale. In the following years Converse expanded his operations by building on the Pacolet River three textile mills which he named Clifton Mills numbers 1, 2, and 3. By the time of his death in 1899, Converse had become the leading textile magnate in the county.

Photograph courtesy of Converse College.

After the phenomenal success of the Glendale Cotton Mill, D. E. Converse wanted to expand his textile manufacturing interests. He bought the site of the South Carolina Iron Works at Clifton in 1880 and built the first of the Clifton Mills. The bridge to the extreme left of the photograph served the workers who lived in the mill village located across the river from the plant. The neat rows of houses above the mill constituted the other half of the village, housing the company's workers.

Photograph courtesy of Stanley Converse.

This Spartanburg County cotton field was photographed about 1900. Although many black residents of the county, both during and after slavery, were skilled artisans, the majority worked in agriculture.

Photograph courtesy of Ned Austell.

Family and employees pose before the McMillin cotton gin in 1904. The girl sitting on the horse in the middle of the picture was the daughter of a Yankee soldier who was part of the Union army stationed in Spartanburg County during Reconstruction. Like so many other Yankees through the years, he had fallen in love with a Southern belle, married her, and settled at Fingerville.

This photograph was taken only two years after a tragedy occurred at this gin. James Henry McMillin, the owner of the gin, was dressed up to go to town but stopped off at the gin to check on the work. When he looked at the gin he saw a piece of lint caught in the blades of the saw, and as so many others have done, he could not resist reaching over to snatch it up. As he did so the blades of the saw caught his cuff link and cut off his arm. He soon died from the accident. Had he been wearing his work clothes he might not have been caught. One of McMillin's descendants comments, "There's such a thing as being too neat."

Photograph courtesy of J. H. McMillin.

67

Mill supervisors in 1902.

The cost of shipping cotton was determined both by the bulk and the weight of the bale. It was important, therefore, to compress as much fiber into a bale as possible. This contraption pressed a bale of about five hundred pounds, which became the standard weight toward the end of the nineteenth century. The old screw cotton press shown here was already outmoded at the time this postcard appeared in 1908.

Courtesy of the South Carolina Museum Commission.

James Alfred Chapman came to Spartanburg from Kentucky in 1899 and built Inman Mill in 1902. The mill contained fifteen thousand spindles and four hundred looms. The mill village was constructed to house workers who came from the mountains of North Carolina and Tennessee and from surrounding towns. The building to the left with the white porch was the company store. Lined up between the houses were the outhouses—the common sanitary facilities of the day. The two boxcars in the photograph illustrate the economic postition of the Southern textile industry. The boxcar in the middle, partially hidden by a building, is from the Southern Railroad and may have just delivered the cotton stacked on the platform behind the mill. The boxcar in front of the company store is part of the Boston and Maine Railroad and is waiting to take finished goods to New York. The textile mills of the South bought their raw materials from their region but sold their manufactured goods to Northern capitalists. Most of the machinery used in the mills also was purchased in the North.

69

Wofford organized its first football team in 1889. After two sucessful contests against Furman, the Wofford faculty criticized the game, and the program languished for a few years. By 1893 Wofford was at it again, playing both Furman and the University of South Carolina. Then came an invitation to play Athens (the University of Georgia) in Spartanburg in 1895. This photograph, taken during that game, shows Athens in the dark jerseys heading for the Wofford goal. Athens won the game 10 to 0, and Wofford moved to hire a regular football coach. Football in those days was so rough that broken bones were not uncommon, and the Methodist Conference of 1896 denounced the game as brutal, criticized it for interfering with scholarship, and forbade it at Wofford. It was not until 1914 that Wofford fielded another football team.

Photograph by Richard F. Peterson; courtesy of Wofford College.

These employees of a Spartanburg County cotton mill assembled for a company photograph in the first decade of the century. The presence of so many young children seems striking in our age, but was common in that day. Serious efforts to curb child labor began in the 1890s, but were resisted both by management and by many workers. Management profited from the lower wages they could pay children, while many parents would have suffered from the decrease in income that child labor legislation would have caused. The children, of course, were not consulted. Some child labor legislation was passed in the first two decades of the century (notably a 1917 law prohibiting employment below the age of fourteen), but the laws were often violated. In 1930 national and state laws set the minimum age at sixteen.

In June 1903 gentle rains fell for nearly five days prior to the torrential downpour on the night of June 6. A worker at one of the Clifton mills became alarmed during the early morning hours at the rapidly rising waters of the Pacolet River, and he gave the alarm. By six o'clock that morning Clifton number 3 was swept downstream against Clifton Mill number 1, and in the chaos more than seventy people died. Pacolet Mills, seen here, was also destroyed, although fewer people in that community lost their lives. The flood swept away bridges, roads, and houses and cut these communities off from the rest of the county. The trolley tracks to Converse, South Carolina were destroyed and were never rebuilt. Two other rivers in the county, the Tyger and the Enoree, also flooded.

Photograph courtesy of Marjorie Atkins.

Clifton Mill number 3 after the flood of 1903.

After the fire of 1892 Converse College immediately rebuilt its Main Building which, in 1903, looked like this.

Photograph courtesy of Ned Austell.

In 1903 the Barnum and Bailey Circus, after five years in Europe, came to Spartanburg for the first time in fifteen years. The circus started with a grand parade which featured "elegant novel allegorical chariot and floats, living tableax, Horses, Elephants and a 40 horse team driven by one man." Thousands of people from all over the piedmont came to Spartanburg to see this truly spectacular show, which boasted over one thousand performers and animals; so large was the circus that it took eighty-six railroad cars in five trains, each about one-half mile long, to transport it. Performances were held just south of Hampton Avenue between South Church and Liberty streets. The photographs give some idea of the crowds that came into town to see the show. People were hanging out of the windows; even the customers of Bishop's Cafe took time out from their "strictly American" food, considered among the best in town, to gape at the spectacle. Bishop's had a marble floor and the reputation to go with it.

Photographs courtesy of H. W. Cudd.

72

Amusements took various forms at the turn of the century. For the affluent, the automobile was a new and fascinating toy which opened up the county to many people on Sunday afternoons. They hoped that it would not rain, for a shower could turn these dirt roads into quagmires. Dr. Hugh R. Black's family is out for a drive in their new Buick. From left to right: Mary Kate Black, Paul Black, Hugh S. Black, Rosa Black, and their mother, Mary Snoddy Black. For Dr. Hugh R. Black the automobile was a welcome tool in getting to his patients quickly.
Photograph courtesy of
Rosa Black.

These four women have just returned from church at the turn of the century. Going to church has always been an important part of the lives of rural people. In addition to its religious aspects, attending church was a time to socialize, to see and be seen, and to dress up, for which people had "Sunday goin' to meetin' " clothes. Although a country phrase, it applied to town people as well. The older woman wears black; around 1900 older women tended to wear black exclusively in mourning for relatives. From left to right: Eliza Sanders, Mrs. Eugene Sanders, Marion Sanders, Toy and May Sanders.
Photograph courtesy of
Ann Sanders Fraser.

Bored with not much to do in 1904, these children built their own trolley. The boys in the back, from left to right, are Theodore and Robbie Richardson; the girls are Carrie Bell Dawkins, Mary Richardson, and Anna Will Sanders.
Photograph courtesy of
Ann Sanders Fraser.

73

When not in class Converse girls early in this century lived in surroundings reminiscent of Sarah Bernhardt. This rather ornate dormitory room was obviously tidied up for the picture, or students of that day were very unlike students of our own. At least there is a picture of college-age men on the table, showing that interests haven't changed all that much.

Photograph courtesy of Converse College.

The Converse campus about 1900. The fountain is surrounded by banana trees. Why banana trees? Note the bicycles just inside the arcade.

Photograph courtesy of Converse College.

These Converse Collge students are boarding the streetcar for an outing in 1906.

Photograph courtesy of Converse College.

The Calhoun and Preston Literary Societies dated from the 1850s and were the most prestigious groups to which a Wofford student could belong. In 1872 the board of trustees made membership in one or the other compulsory. The societies engaged in long debates, some of which became quite acrimonious. Although for a time some students treated membership with indifference, for the most part students took the activities of the societies seriously. The halls seem to invite the serious, if not the ponderous. This is the Calhoun Society Hall in 1909.
Photograph courtesy of Wofford College.

The Preston Literary Society Hall in 1909.
Photograph courtesy of Wofford College.

The athletic association of Converse College inaugurated May Day festivities in 1910. The pageant included dancing, singing, and a drama, all centered around a special theme. A May queen was crowned, and people came from the city to watch the festivities. The event continues to this day.
Photograph, 1916, courtesy of Converse College

Around 1900 the city of Spartanburg spent a great deal of money on its streets. By paving some streets and curbing and making sidewalks on others, the city fathers hoped to enhance the progressive reputation of the area. This view of West Main Street looking west was taken from a point just beyond the Opera House. The granite stone for the curbing came from a quarry off to the right at the bottom of the hill just behind where the Steeple Drive-In is located today. The building to the left was a feed and sale stable owned by L. E. Castleberry and P. J. White. Next to that was an establishment that bought bottles. The house on the top of the hill to the left belonged to A. J. Gwynn, who was a real estate broker. The Western and Carolina Railroad ran at the base of the hill. The house on the extreme right with the tall columns belonged to Fielding Cantrell, who sold buggies and wagons in a shop next door, about where the photographer is standing. Cantrell's shop stands there to this day next door to the Masonic Lodge across from the Herald Journal building. The boarding house in the photograph was known as the Carolina House and was owned by Miss M. T. Lipscomb. Into the twentieth century it was not unusual to find businesses and residences—some very nice ones—side by side. It was the automobile and the trolley which made it possible to develop areas strictly for housing and others devoted only to business.

Photograph by Bernhardt; courtesy of the Spartanburg County Historical Association.

Taken prior to 1903, this photograph of West Main Street looking east toward town shows the condition of streets at the time. The woman trudging up the hill illustrates what it must have been like to walk to town for your shopping before Spartanburg's hills were cut down. The pipes on the left indicate that the street crews were trying to alleviate the washing problem that plagued the town. In the distance stands the tower of the Opera House and just to the right of it, partially hidden behind an electric pole, stands the Beehive, a department store.

Photograph by Bernhardt; courtesy of the Spartanburg County Historical Association.

In this 1905 picture of Morgan Square, Greenewald's has moved out of the Duncan Building and True's department store has moved in. True's opened for business in 1905, saying it would sell quality merchandise for the lowest prices Spartanburg had ever seen. True's advertised that the store bought for cash and expected to sell for cash. The opening of a new department store was news in itself, but True's had an extra attraction—the first elevator in Spartanburg. Floyd Liles had installed the elevator when he operated a store here, but True's made the most of the novelty by bringing people in "just for the ride." It did not hurt business. To the left of True's, just across Magnolia Street, is the First National Bank, and farther down the street the Spartan Inn and the Opera House. This is one of the last pictures of the Opera House before the opening under the tower was boarded up. The building was torn down in 1907.

Postcard view courtesy of the Spartanburg Herald-Journal.

As part of the extensive and expensive program to improve the streets between 1890 and 1910, these workers are laying "vitrified" brick in Morgan Square in 1900. This glasslike surface was considered the most advanced and beautiful paving material in that day, and its appearance led some citizens to refer to Morgan Square as a "courtyard." Whether said in jest or not, almost anything was an improvement over the sea of mud that for years had brought everything to a standstill on wet days. In 1882 the city had macadamized (packed small broken stone on a roadbed) some streets only to find that dirt stuck to them with a vengeance. By 1900 the macadam had been completely covered with a thick layer of dirt. Vitrified brick was considered superior to macadam because mud washed off the former when it rained.

Photograph courtesy of
Wofford College.

Although not a beauty, Samuel T. Poinier was a veteran of many heated political contests, all of which he managed to survive. Appointed postmaster during Reconstruction, he was time and time again the target of post-Reconstruction efforts to remove him from office. The determination with which he met each challenge shows through in this turn-of-the-century photograph.

Courtesy of the
Spartanburg County
Historical Association.

The crowd at the Southern Depot on Magnolia Street attests to the importance of rail travel at the turn of the century. Spartanburg was unusual in that two Southern Railway main lines converged here at Union Station. Passengers could go in any of the four compass directions from Spartanburg. The trains would be sitting side by side in front of the station, and a mad scramble would take place as passengers changed trains or simply tried to board the right train. The presence of the Charleston and Western Carolina trains on the other side of the station only added to the confusion. The feeling was not unlike the sensations shared by passengers at one of our major airports.

Photograph courtesy of the
Spartanburg County
Historical Association.

These Spartanburg beauties were
photographed about 1900.

Photograph courtesy of
Dexter Cleveland.

Photograph courtesy of
Charlie Mae Campbell Family.

Photograph courtesy of
Dexter Cleveland.

John Gary Evans, former governor of South Carolina, built this residence in Converse Heights for $9,900 in 1901. It is presently the residence of Judge Donald Russell.

Photograph by James Buchanan; Courtesy of the Aug. W. Smith Company.

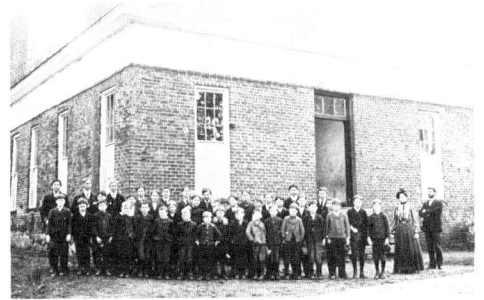

It is not very often that preachers see quick and practical results from their sermons. But in 1857 the Reverend R. H. Reid of Nazareth Church preached a sermon on the importance of education, and a few months later that congregation established a school for males. A village was laid out (the first effort at urban planning in the county) with the male school at one end of the main street and the female school, established in 1859, at the other. The trustees elected Reverend Reid to head the schools, and he served in that capacity for forty years. Throughout the county the Reidville schools had a well-deserved reputation for scholarship, and colleges were pleased to enroll their graduates. Professor J. L. McWhorter and his sister stand here with their pupils in 1903.

Photograph by J. M. Taylor; courtesy of the Spartanburg County Historical Association.

The country store was the focal point of any rural community. The variety of goods it carried made it the earliest of department stores, and its usually small space and corner wood stove made it a place for gathering and exchanging tales and woes. In some ways the precursor of the modern convenience store, a country store could keep a farm family going a long time before a trip into town would become necessary. Cloth, hardware, and food made the country store a place of joy and sometimes heartbreak, for farm families often had needs their resources could not meet. This is Poole's in Enoree around 1900.

Photograph courtesy of Ron Lanford.

81

Until 1906, when the Opera House was destroyed, people who wanted to photograph Morgan Square stood on the eastern end and took a picture looking west; thus the photographer was facing the Morgan monument with the picturesque Spartan Inn and Opera House in the background. Because of this tendency, no other pictures are available of the Opera House alone. Unfortunately, by the time this picture was taken the arcade had been boarded up in preparation for demolition. The Opera House had red walls and a blue ceiling in its theater, which could seat about eight hundred people. The demands for entertainment in the city were growing, and the seating capacity of the Opera House was too small to accommodate the crowds. But the manager of the theater, Max Greenewald, of Greenewald's clothing store, brought entertainment to the people up to one month before the building was torn down. There was a show almost every night, except Sundays, from the fall through the spring. The shows ranged from A Message From Mars (with novel electrical effects) and East Lynne (for which the Herald reported standing room was sold, and many turned away), to Parsifal (presumably the opera by Wagner).

Photograph courtesy of
Wofford College.

In 1903 in the east half of the building on the corner of West Main and South Church streets Harry Price opened his store for men. Price catered to a middle-class trade, advertising that he sought to fill the "wants of every gentleman so far as they pertain to Man's Furnishings." He did so by offering shirts from fifty cents to a dollar-fifty, neckwear from twenty-five cents to seventy-five cents, and men's straw hats from thirty-five cents to three dollars. Harry Price stands before his store in 1904 on the right of the photograph next to his dog, Lucille.

Photograph courtesy of
Harry Price.

The interior of Ezell's hardware store around 1900.
Photograph courtesy of Ned Austell.

Samuel B. Ezell, the bearded man, stands before his hardware store with his employees. Perhaps the man on the right with the bowler and the briefcase was passing by and stopped to be included, or he might have been a salesman. Ezell operated his store in the Spartan Inn, so this photograph was taken before 1910.
Photograph courtesy of B & B Studio.

Until 1910 hotels in the immediate vicinity of Union Station on Magnolia Street were small and inferior to the larger establishments around Morgan Square. Then the Gresham was built to cater especially to passengers, itinerant salesmen, and other business people seeking lodging near the station. The Gresham (later called the Morgan) stood directly across the street from Union Station and was, in its heyday, one of Spartanburg's finest hotels. The Gresham eventually became, as so many downtown hotels have, a victim of the decline of rail travel.

R. O. Pickens came to Spartanburg and started his roofing business in the old Spartan Inn in 1904. Pickens, second from the left, and his crew set out on a job.
Photograph courtesy of R. O. and B. R. Pickens.

The United States Post Office was built in 1906 on North Church Street across the street from the present site of the Montgomery Building. The post office was destroyed in mid-century.
Photograph courtesy of B & B Studio.

Spartanburg's first city hospital, now the Georgia Cleveland Home.
Photograph by Linda Taylor Hudgins.

Spartanburg people visited local springs for relaxation, for walks on wooded paths, and sometimes for medicinal qualities which actually were or were merely perceived to be in the water. One such place was Kirby Springs, later known as White Stone Spring because of the white mineral coating on the exposed rock. Note the continuously flowing water to the left in this circa-1900 photograph of a Sunday outing. From left to right: Jones Foster, James C. Foster, Lula Foster, Neynon Fowler, and Lloyd Dillard.

Photograph courtesy of the Spartanburg Herald-Journal.

Glendale Park was part of the mill community of Glendale. Its woods and pond were a pleasant place to picnic and to spend an afternoon. In 1900 a trolley line was opened from Spartanburg through Glendale to the Clifton Mills. The line ran up East Main Street down Pine Street to Country Club Road, where it turned off to Glendale. After 1900 a trip to Glendale Park was often part of a city school teacher's reward to her students for a job well done. A family outing to Glendale Park was an inexpensive and pleasant activity for mill worker and executive alike.

Photograph courtesy of the Spartanburg County Historical Association.

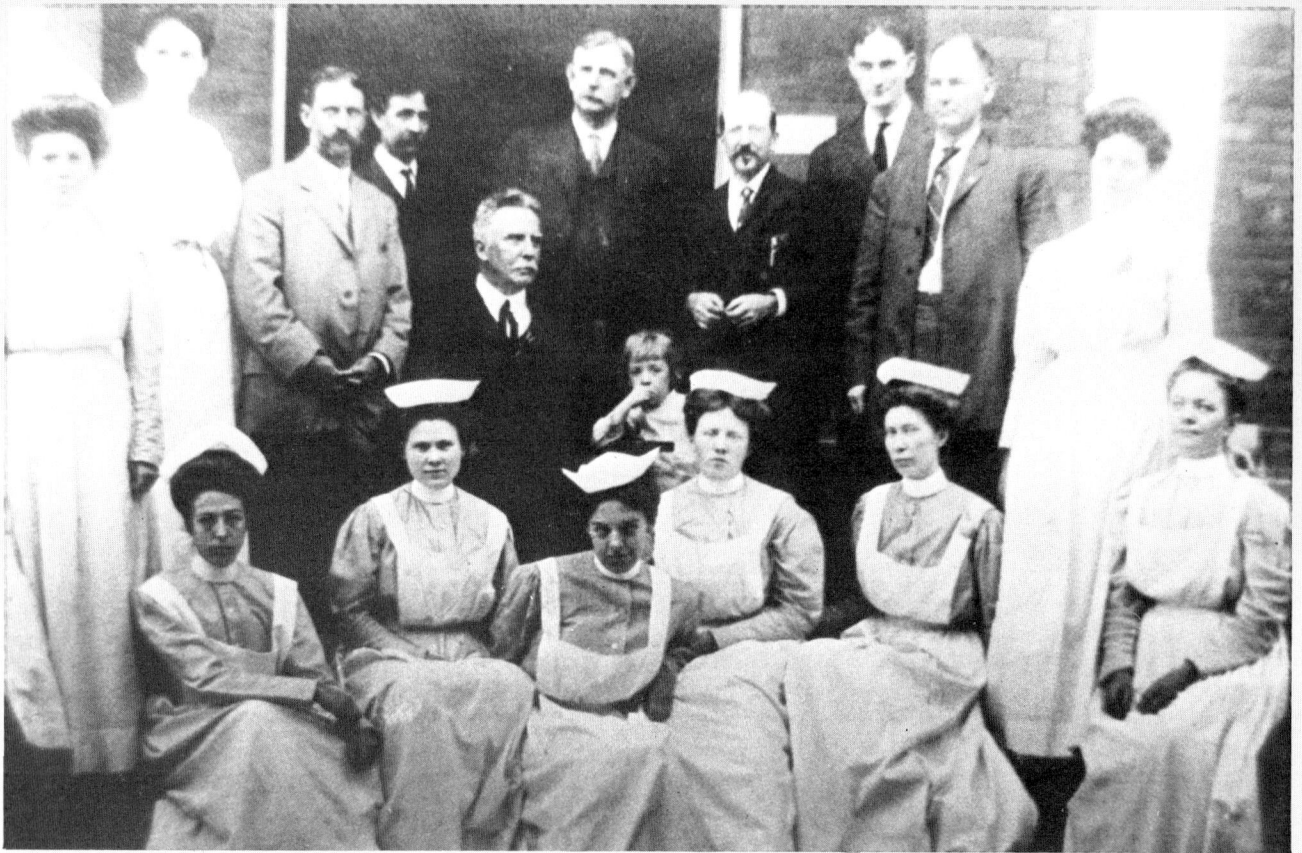

Photograph courtesy of Marianna Black Habisreutinger.

In 1904 Drs. Black, Jefferies, and Heinitsh seeking better places to do surgery than kitchen tables, bought a house on North Dean Street and founded the Spartanburg Hospital. In 1907 they built Spartanburg's first structure specifically designed as a hospital, next door to their building on North Dean Street. Later this hospital was sold to John B. Cleveland, who deeded it to the trustees for the establishment of a home for aged women, known as the Georgia Cleveland Home. This photograph shows the doctors who were stockholders and practitioners in the Spartanburg Hospital along with the head of nursing and her staff. From left to right in the top row: Lena K. Sharp, head nurse; Dr. R. A. Fike; Dr. James L. Jeffries; Dr. George R. Dean; Dr. Hugh Ratchford Black; Dr. George Heinitsh; Dr. W. A. Wallace; Dr. Joe Allen. The young boy is Edwin W. Johnson.

Rock Cliff Park opened in 1910. It was located at what used to be called Garrett Springs and close to an old mill. The park stood off Heywood Avenue near the bridge over Lawson's Fork, and unlike other parks of the time, it provided a Ferris wheel, a merry-go-round, and a ride called the "ocean wave." This latter contraption turned around while lifting and dropping the occupant much like a wave would do. For the adults there was a bowling alley, a dance pavilion, and facilities for swimming and boating. The trolley ran up East Main Street to the park. Nothing remains of the park today except the very end of the trolley tracks.

Of the things to do and the places to go at the turn of the century, perhaps the most exciting continued to be, as it had been for so long, a trip to Glenn Springs. But getting there was made much easier after 1894 when the picturesque Glenn Springs Railroad opened. The train ran from Roebuck to Glenn Springs, a nine-mile trip. Coming from Spartanburg, passengers would board a Charleston and Western Carolina train at the Union depot and ride out to Roebuck where they would connect with the little two-car Glenn Springs train. Many important people came to the resort every summer, and the train service was first rate. The conductor, Captain Tom Smith, was a handsome man who stood about six feet, three inches, and who drove a two-horse carriage to work every day. In this photograph he is leaning out the doorway of the baggage car, immediately behind the engine. The engineer was Giles Templeton and the fireman was Mr. Miller, both of whom are standing in the engine compartment. The porter, Joe Clark, stands just to the left of the man leaning against the train. The train from Roebuck cost adults seventy-five cents and children thirty-five cents. The captain was known to "neglect" to collect from children who were residents of Glenn Springs and who often liked to ride the train.

In his digging around Spartanburg, for which he is well known, Bill Littlejohn found this medal awarded by the Spartanburg Horse Show Association in 1911.

Medal courtesy of
William B. Littlejohn;
photograph by Linda Taylor Hudgins.

For twenty years, beginning in 1890, the Woodruff fair drew people from the southern half of the county. The fairs lasted three days and were held in the fall when the weather was cool. There were exhibits, a grandstand, and the most popular of all, a racetrack. The half-mile track provided spectators not only with the fast sulky races shown in this photograph made about 1907, but also with riding contests among the women, in the ring in the middle of the track. Riding sidesaddle, the ladies paced their horses at a walk, hoping to impress the judges with their ability and style.

Photograph courtesy of
Ron Lanford.

Hotel hacks working Union Station about 1910. In the heyday of rail travel it was customary for hotel porters to pick up passengers and their luggage at the train station.

Photograph courtesy of the
Spartanburg County
Historical Association.

This 1912 photograph of the Glenn Springs train gives some indication of the popularity of the resort. The boy standing on the steps is James Zimmerman, a resident of Glenn Springs.

Photograph courtesy of the
Spartanburg Herald-Journal.

Ann Sanders Fraser was photographed on her Marsh Tacky Pidgin, which in 1909 meant a little horse. Ann had typhoid fever and in her delirium she talked incessantly about riding a horse. Her father, grateful that she recovered, bought her the horse in Charleston. Sanders' law partner, Harry De Pass, persuaded Sanders to permit Ann to ride "astride" because riding side-saddle was too dangerous. Ann thus became the first girl in the area to ride astride.

Photograph courtesy of
Ann Sanders Fraser.

A snow in 1905 brought out topcoats and furs. The camera also brought out Donald Sanders, the young boy in the background, who, according to Sanders family tradition, managed to get into every picture the family took. From left to right: Ann and Marion Sanders, Mary and Theodore Richardson.

Photograph courtesy of
Ann Sanders Fraser.

At 3:30 a.m. on April 22, 1910, a clerk discovered a fire behind R. O. Pickens' shop in the Spartan Inn. Firefighters battled the blaze for five hours in heat so intense that plate glass windows across Morgan Square broke. Gunpowder in S. B. Ezell's hardware store on the street level of the inn was barely removed before the flames got to it. The building burned to the ground, and John B. Cleveland, who owned two-thirds interest in the structure, said the next day that he had carried very little insurance on the property because the rates were too high. Shopowners whose businesses had been located in the building reported the same reluctance to carry the expensive coverage. The fire deprived the city of Spartanburg of one of its most picturesque buildings and one of the very last structures which had made up the "old Morgan Square."

Photograph by Alfred T. Willis;
courtesy of the
Aug. W. Smith Company.

Main Street running from Liberty through Morgan Square was the main business street in the city until the 1960s. Even at 9:00 a.m. East Main Street looked busy in 1912. Today the clock tower stands in the middle of what was Liberty Street in the Main Street Mall. In 1912 the two top floors of the building on the extreme left—which still stands—comprised Dr. Benjamin B. Steedly's Private Hospital, and the bottom floor was Nicholas Trakas' fruit store. The white railroad crossing barriers behind the automobile on the left were located at the Southern Railway crossing, and the Bee Hive was a department store. The vertical "drugs" sign in the distance on the left was the Central Drug Company, which was located across Church Street. The clock on the right belonged to Crosby's Jewelers; just beyond it was Paul and Leroy Dunbar's shop where they repaired, built, and sold wagons. The wagons on the right with the horses who would not keep still for the photographer were probably owned by people seeking help in Dunbar's shop. Dunbar Street, which is one block to the right running parallel to Main, was named for the men who worked there.

The pickup truck, the sedan, and the pedestrians standing on the trolley tracks foreshadow the coming age. This photograph was taken at the corner of East Main and Church streets in 1910.
Photograph by Alfred T. Willis; courtesy of the Aug. W. Smith Company.

The Spartanburg Country Club opened in 1910 in this building. According to some old-time residents, the city enjoyed a tennis boom about that time, and the country club was popular because it furnished some of the better courts in town. Shortly after the country club opened, the county went dry and many members were sadly disappointed.
Postcard view courtesy of the Spartanburg Herald-Journal.

Converse College has a long tradition of serving the musical needs of Spartanburg. From almost the very beginning of the school it has devoted much of its resources to building a fine school of music. In 1895 R. H. Peters, the director of music at Converse, and Albert Twitchell founded the Festival of Music. Converse named its auditorium for Twitchell in recognition of his contribution to the music of Spartanburg. This photograph shows the elegance of the hall in 1910.
Photograph courtesy of Wofford College.

The interior of the Dunbar Brothers' Carriage Shop on East Main Street looked like this in 1900.
Photograph courtesy of Ned Austell.

This view of Trade Street when it was not much more than an alley was taken about 1912. The photographer was looking toward Dunbar Street from Elm (Saint John). The building on the left with the letters "ON" on the side was the Weddington Harware Company, and just beyond was Thad C. Dean's feed store. Dean advertised in the newspapers constantly, once claiming: "I have a car of choice Timothy Hay, the best ever—It will make the 'horse laugh.'" Trade Street was the birthplace of a number of Spartanburg businesses, among them C. L. Cannon Company and the Community Cash stores owned by Broadus Littlejohn.

Alley From St John St to W Parking lot — Now between St John & Commerce St "TRADE St"

Following the construction of the Magnolia Street School in 1889, the city struggled valiantly to provide enough space to educate all its children. The attempt was marked by the construction of buildings so formidable that they looked as if they would keep the children in and the parents out. They were like fortresses—veritable "citadels of learning." The old Southside School, built in 1906, eventually became Jenkins Junior High School, which was torn down in the 1970s.

Photograph by Alfred T. Willis.

Established in 1886, Greenewald's has been serving the clothing needs of the men of Spartanburg ever since. Shortly after 1892, Greenewald's located in the Duncan Building on the north side of Morgan Square at the corner of Magnolia Street, but it soon moved over to the south side of the square. In 1910 it moved to the corner of South Church and West Main streets, where it remains to this day. At the time this picture was taken in 1911, Greenewald's was the second store west of Church; part of the building was later removed to widen South Church Street. Max Greenewald, third from the left in the picture, was an active citizen, for he was involved both in volunteer firefighting and in running the entertainments at the old Opera House. The clerks in the photograph are, from left to right: unknown, Clyde Whitlock, Max Greenewald, E. W. Miller, J. L. Trimmier, and Milton C. Lancaster. Note the ninety-nine cent pants, the bowler hats in the glass cases to the left, the collars next to Lancaster, and the elaborate trunk on the floor between the tables on the left. Such sturdy trunks were a necessity for touring in that day.

Photograph courtesy of James D. Cobb.

The city of Spartanburg had two schoolhouses by the 1890s. In addition to the Magnolia Street School the city operated a school on North Converse Street. By 1910 the latter had become a boarding house run by Virginia Brewton, who stands here on the left with her boarders and cook. It was quite common in the nineteenth and early twentieth centuries for widows to take in young ladies to live with them. It helped with expenses, gave the widows company, filled up all the space in those big houses, and prevented a social taboo: young women were not supposed to live by themselves; they had to be under the protection and guidance of a suitable older woman.

Photograph courtesy of
Rosa Black.

When construction began on the Chapman Building (later known as the Andrews Building) there was an air of excitement in the community. Spartans had only read about skyscrapers in the larger cities of the north, yet now they would have one of their own. The anticipation turned out to be fully justified, for the Chapman Building was a beautiful addition to the center of the city and a worthy heir to the grace which had been endangered by the loss since 1890 of many buildings along the square.

Photograph by Alfred T. Willis;
courtesy of the
Aug. W. Smith Company.

The overpass is believed to be one built by the Piedmont and Northern Railway going westward to Greenville. The time is about 1910. That someone would take the trouble to photograph his spouse or girlfriend at such a place indicates the pride with which Spartans viewed their railroad expansion.

Photograph courtesy of the
Spartanburg County Historical
Association.

The Oakland Avenue School was built in 1911. It was torn down in the 1950s. Photograph by Alfred T. Willis.

Sometime between 1900 and 1914 the Spartanburg Police Department stood for this portrait in front of the old jail built in 1823. The jail was torn down in 1914 to make way for a new city hall. Lionel Lawson tells the following about Sergeant S. J. Alverson, standing in this picture in the first row on the extreme left. It seems that Alverson arrested two men for driving an automobile on the sidewalk from the First Baptist Church to Liberty Street. They protested the arrest saying, "Sergeant Alverson, now you aren't going to arrest us for a little thing like this are you?" Alverson responded, "Now you boys know better than that; I'll have to take you in for an offense as serious as this one." When the two appeared before Mayor John Floyd, he asked them why they had done such a foolish thing. "Well Mr. Mayor, I just bought that brand new Chalmers automobile, and it was just too good to ride in the street along with all them other cars." The mayor dismissed the case with a wry smile.

Photograph courtesy of the Spartanburg Herald-Journal.

Cotton gin workers aboard "King Cotton" in 1910.
Photograph courtesy of R. H. McMillin.

The nursing program at the old city hospital provided Spartanburg with qualified trained nurses for many years. Here in 1917 several trainees show that such a life was not all work, although they did have to live in special quarters next door to the hospital (the Georgia Cleveland Home) under rather rigid rules.
Photograph courtesy of Rosa Black.

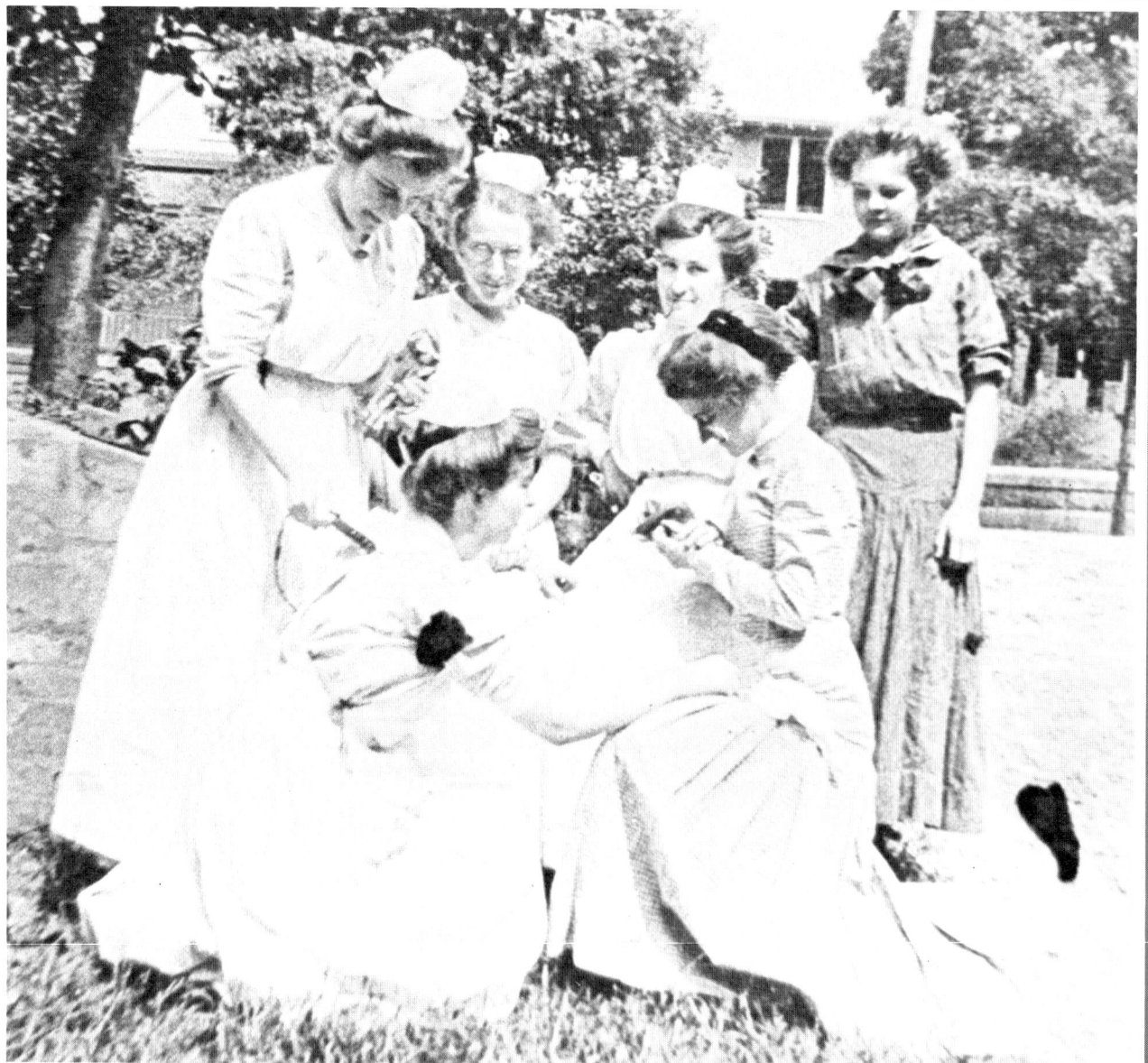

Hattie Gentry had shown off her hair in the 1870s, and her daughter, Hattie Weste Harris, did the same in 1910.
Photograph courtesy of Jennie Rhinehart.

In 1791 the state of South Carolina had granted Andrew McMillin 394 acres of land in the Fingerville area. Over the years the McMillins started various businesses, most of which were located just southeast of Fingerville on the North Pacolet River. Early in the nineteenth century they built a small building, attached to the three-story structure to the left of the picture, as a grist mill powered by Obed Creek, which runs under the bridge shown here. Later, the three-story structure was built as a wheat mill, but Obed Creek did not provide the necessary power to drive the large water wheel. Therefore, the McMillins dammed the North Pacolet River, which was off to the top right of the picture, and built a sluice to the wheat mill to power the wheel. By the time this photograph was taken in 1910, neither mill was in operation. The building behind the wheat mill was a cotton warehouse, but it was not large enough to store all the bales, and the overflow can be seen in the yard. Leaving cotton out in the weather was common among Southern ginners. The house was the McMillin residence at the time, and the small cabin to the extreme right of the picture was an old blacksmith shop. Here, in one picture, is a miniature history of the activities of ambitious Spartanburg farmers. Corn and wheat mills, cotton gins and blacksmith's shops were the mainstays of much of the county's economy in the nineteenth century.

Photograph courtesy of R. H. McMillin.

Except for the organ on the right, the interior of this mill village house was typical. The photograph was taken in 1913.
Courtesy of the South Caroliniana Library.

School children stand before the elementary school provided for them in a cotton mill village in the late teens.
Photograph courtesy of Elisabeth Bridgeman Jones.

Pellagra, a chronic disease which was the scourge of thousands of Spartanburg County residents early in this century, was characterized by boils, stomach trouble, and general listlessness. There were two schools of thought in the scientific community on the cause of the problem: some believed that the cause was poor sanitary conditions, but others believed that it was inadequate diet. Diet was largely discounted because the disease occurred in the summer when a variety of foods was available, but few suspected that it took some six months for a dietary deficiency to manifest itself. In 1913 the United States' Public Health Service chose Spartanburg County as one of the areas in which to conduct studies of the disease. These pictures of typical mill village and farm dwellings were taken by the investigators in 1913 to illustrate sanitary and general living conditions among those people in the county most prone to contract the disease. Eventually, it was discovered that diet was the cause of pellagra; in the winter months people ate white corn meal, sow belly, molasses, grits, and rice. White gravy and biscuits were a must with almost every meal, but people ate few vegetables and got few vitamins.
Courtesy of the South Caroliniana Library.

Typical farmhouse and well, 1913.
Photograph courtesy of the
South Caroliniana Library.

Negro tenant farmhouse, 1913.
Photograph courtesy of the
South Caroliniana Library.

A shift in a cotton mill had its photograph taken in 1915. Notice that the children are barefoot, the cause of the rampant spread of hookworm. Around 1910 Walter Hines Page of North Carolina waged a newspaper war against two ever-present conditions of life for poor Southerners—poor sanitary conditions and bare feet. He wanted to rid Southerners of hookworm, but their politicians and newspaper editors became defensive and attacked Page as a traitor to the region for even suggesting the presence of the parasite among them. If some of the mill workers of the time look debilitated, the cause was not only long working hours and poor diet but also the frequent infestation of hookworm brought about by filthy outhouses and the lack of shoes, both conditions caused by poverty and ignorance.

Photograph courtesy of
Elisabeth Bridgeman Jones.

Wells in mill villages in the county in 1913.

Photograph courtesy of the South Caroliniana Library.

Just after the turn of the century Spartanburg was the site of many conventions, and one of the largest was that held for Shriners from the southeastern states in 1911. For the occasion Robert Olin Pickens built this marvelous camel based on the Dromedary date package. Some boys pulled the animal along the street on bicycle wheels. Pickens constructed the camel out of copper, angle irons, and cowhide; it took him two months to build, and he was paid $186 for the job. The best part of the construction was the special use to which it was put. Pickens made the hump removable, and a keg of beer could be placed inside with 250 pounds of ice. The saddlebags held paper cups, and when the faucet connected to the udder was turned, the red light bulbs in the eyes would light up. After the convention the camel went on display in the Harris theater and was then shipped to the west coast for another convention. It never came back.

Photograph courtesy of R. O. and B. R. Pickens.

Confererate Veterans celebrate in front of the courthouse.

Courtesy of the Spartanburg County Historical Association.

Confederate veterans from all over the South gathered in Spartanburg in 1910 for a reunion. They crowded the streetcars, held parades and celebrations in front of the courthouse, and gathered for picnics. Spartanburg celebrated the event in a special way by placing a Confederate monument on Kirby Hill at the intersection of what is today South Church and Henry streets. In 1910 Kirby Hill was at least four feet higher than it is today. In the mid-twentieth century the monument was moved to the American Legion Home in Duncan Park because it was considered a traffic hazard in its old location.

Courtesy of the Spartanburg County Historical Association.

In 1912 East Main Street was a lovely residential area from Liberty Street going east. The photographer caught these linemen working at the corner of East Main and Liberty. The houses from right to left belonged to Harry Price, Dr. L. J. Blake, and J. B. Lee, the mayor of Spartanburg.

Courtesy of the Spartanburg County Historical Association.

A view of East Main Street taken about 1914 from the roof of the Herzog Apartment House. The Chapman Building is visible in the distance. Looking right from the Greenewald's sign are the residences of Robert and James Chapman, the First Presbyterian Church, and Mrs. M. L. Flynn's boarding house. The large white house just right of Converse Street is Mrs. C. L. Cannon's house, the finest boarding house in the city. The trolley tracks and the wires for the electric trolley cars can be seen running down East Main Street.

Photograph courtesy of Marshall Chapman.

Salvation Army workers took a few minutes to have their photograph taken in 1914 before they delivered their annual Christmas baskets. Photograph courtesy of Rosa Black.

By 1915 East Main Street had undergone some changes. The Southern Bell Telephone office was located above the Elite Ice Cream Parlor, and F. W. Woolworth Company had moved in next to Kress. Just beyond the Southern Railway crossing the Grand movie house had opened in 1913. The trees just beyond the last building on the left begin the residential portion of Main Street. The building in which Kress is located was the Argyle Hotel. As in the other, older hotels in the city, the Argyle had shops (a barber shop, a pool room, and Kress') on the street level and its guests rooms on the upper floors.

Photograph courtesy of the Spartanburg Herald-Journal.

The Argyle Hotel dining room about 1905.

Photograph courtesy of Wofford College.

TEXTILE INSTITUTE. SPARTANBURG. S. C.

In 1911 David English Camak, a Methodist preacher, opened a school primarily for the children of mill workers. Under the Camak plan a child worked two weeks and used his earnings to attend school for two weeks. The children were paired so that work in the mill could continue uninterrupted. By 1913 Camak had this building and his success was assured. The Textile Industrial Institute grew into Spartanburg Methodist College.

Photograph courtesy of Wofford College.

The Elite (pronounced "a-leet") became the most popular eating place in the city from the 1920s through the 1950s. Nicholas Trakas, the man with the mustache, had a fruit stand on East Main Street for years before he decided to put some tables in and serve food. Soon the Elite drew a steady clientele who liked not only to eat but also to talk. The first man on the left is George Harakas. The photograph was taken in 1914 when the Elite first began to serve food and had just installed a soda fountain.

Photograph by Alfred T. Willis; courtesy of Nicholas Harakas.

In 1914 the Southern Bell switchboard was located above the Elite on East Main Street.

Photograph courtesy of the Spartanburg Herald-Journal.

The Imperial Hotel in Landrum was one of the better known "country hotels" in the county in 1913. The building has been demolished.

Augustus W. Smith, a textile executive living in Woodruff, bought a store in his home town of Abbeville, South Carolina, in 1890. By 1901 he decided to move the store to Spartanburg and sold Frank McGee, the store's manager, a one-half interest in the business to get him to come to Spartanburg and manage the business here. The Aug. W. Smith Company opened a store on East Main Street where Belk's is presently located. In 1925 McGee and city officials made a deal that if the store were to move farther east on Main Street the city would widen the roadway from Liberty to Pine. So the Aug. W. Smith Company purchased the Chapman property and built its new store where it stands today. Meanwhile Smith had moved to Spartanburg and built a house at the corner of East Main Street and Mills Avenue, which now serves as the Converse College Alumnae House. In later years, Smith moved to Greenville, South Carolina, to pursue his primary career in textiles. When this photograph was taken in 1912, Price's store for men was next door, and between the two can be seen a display case for collars, a major item in men's wear.

Photograph by Alfred T. Willis; courtesy of the Aug. W. Smith Company.

109

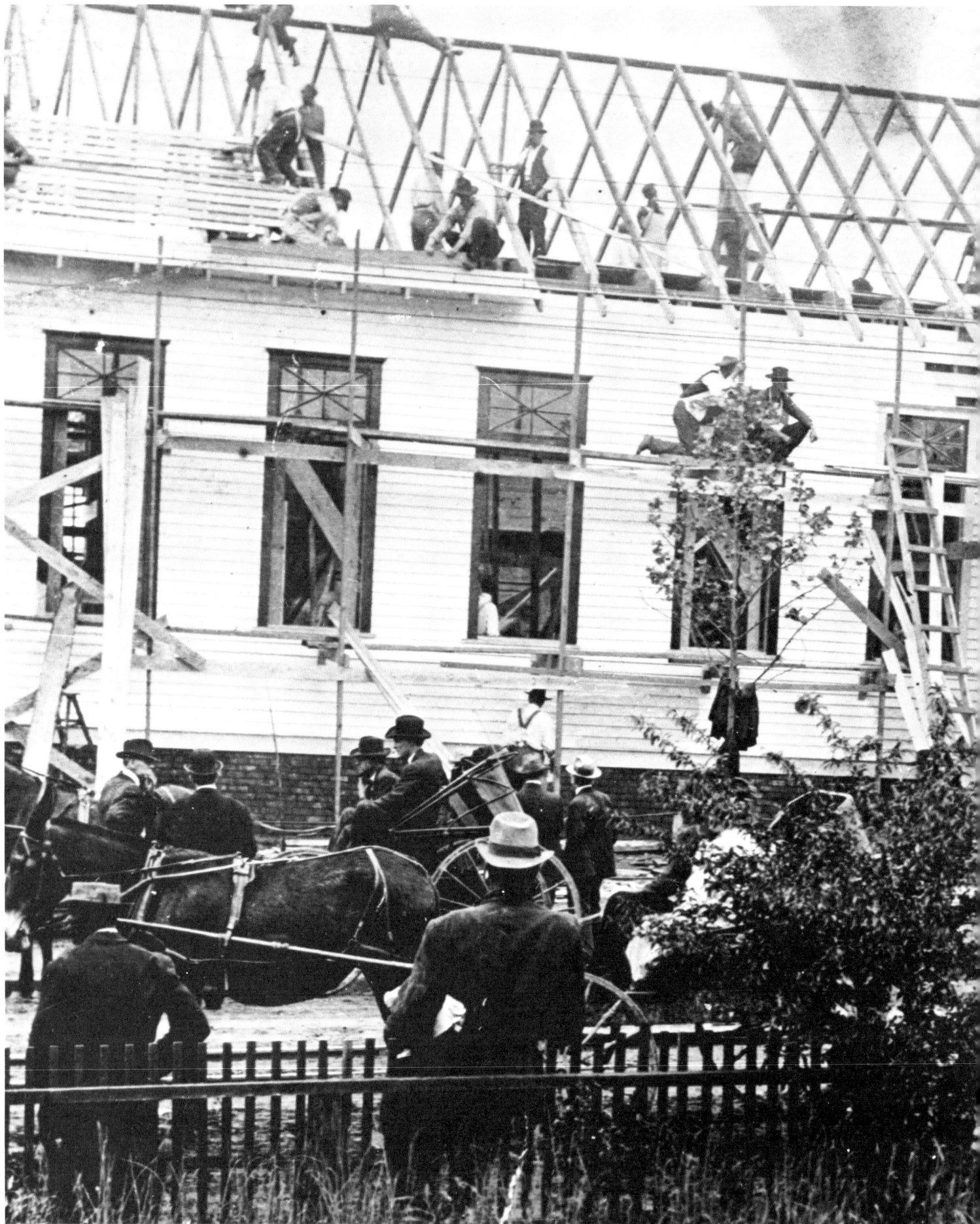

In 1914 the old county jail, made of soapstone and field rocks, was destroyed in order to build the city hall, shown here with later additions to the left. The city hall stood approximately where the present city hall now stands in front of Wall Street. Before 1914 Wall Street was known as Jail Street.

Photograph courtesy of B & B Studio.

After the turn of the century members of the congregation of Bethel Methodist Church became aware that people who lived farther down South Church Street had difficulty in coming to services. Although there had been much talk, no action had ever been taken. In 1912 Charles P. Hammond, the owner of a furniture store in Spartanburg and a man of action, decided that a new church must be built to serve the South Church Street population. Hammond arranged for carpenters, plumbers, roofers, painters, and brickmasons to arrive at the site for the new church on the first day of May at 7:00 a.m. The men worked furiously throughout the day, with no pay, and by evening the new congregation held its first service in the completed church. Although it had been known ever since in the community as the "One-Day Church," the building was officially named El Bethel after its parent congregation. The structure was replaced in mid-century.

Photograph courtesy of B & B Studio.

111

These people are waiting in line for the first tickets to the South Atlantic Music Festival in 1912. Patrons spent six dollars for five performances. The man in the bowler hat at the front of the line was W. S. Glenn who, for several years, came early to be the first to buy the much-sought-after tickets.

Photograph courtesy of B & B Studio.

Peter Joseph McCauley came to South Carolina from Ireland and settled in Boiling Springs. A Roman Catholic, McCauley took his children to Spartanburg for services in the Catholic church every Sunday, no matter the condition of the roads or the weather.

Being a Roman Catholic put McCauley in a small minority in Spartanburg County, but he showed his Irish pluck by wearing a cross around his waist. His seven children (the little girl leaning against the porch was a neighbor) seem to share their father's dash as they pose outside their house about 1910. From left to right: Peter, Bennie, James, Paul, Annie, John, William, unknown, Agnes, and Mary.

Photograph courtesy of Mrs. Maury Pearson, Jr.

112

The Jewish Temple, B'nai Israel, was built in 1916 at the intersection of Dean and Union streets opposite Evans High School. The building was sold about 1960 and a new temple built on Heywood Avenue.

The Cleveland Hotel was built in 1915 where the west end of the old Spartan Inn had stood. The hotel was named the Cleveland because the property had belonged to John B. Cleveland, and it stood directly in front of the site where Jesse Cleveland had built his store in 1810. The Cleveland was the largest of the city's overnight accommodations.

Photograph courtesy of the Spartanburg Herald-Journal.

This typical, small turn-of-the-century house on North Fairview bordering Converse College is no longer standing. Bicycles and tricycles were very popular items about the town in 1915 when this photograph was taken.

Courtesy of Converse College.

Dr. Benjamin B. Steedly built this private hospital in 1916 on the north side of East Main Street between Alabama Street and Oakland Avenue. In the mid-1920s the Young Women's Christian Association took over most of the building because a new city hospital had been constructed on North Church Street. Later the building was turned into apartments, and it was torn down in 1960.
Photograph courtesy of B & B Studio.

By 1915 cannons and cannon balls as well as an iron fence to keep children and vehicles away from the pedestal had been added to Morgan's statue.

Trolley cars were in their heyday. The trolley in the middle is coming from Magnolia Street and the other, on the right, is headed for East Main Street.

Photograph by Alfred T. Willis; courtesy of the Aug. W. Smith Company.

In its heyday the Cleveland Hotel was rather posh, as this 1918 postcard of the terrace illustrates.
Courtesy of the South Carolina Historical Museum.

North Church Street looked like this about 1910. The Central National Bank would eventually move into the Andrews Building. The steeple in the distance belongs to Central Methodist Church.

The city of Spartanburg once had an electric trolley system of which any town its size could have been proud. The system eventually ran from Union Station on Magnolia eastward up Main Street, north and south on Church Street, then past Converse College to Rock Cliff Park. The trolley could turn south on Pine Street (there was no North Pine until the 1950s) to the Country Club Road, where the car proceeded to Glendale, Clifton and Converse. This service began about 1900 and continued into the 1920s, at which time a struggle broke out between the city and the owners of the trolley company. Since about 1916 the street railway had been losing money, and it wanted to curtail service drastically. There ensued one of the longest and most spectacular transportation franchise fights in American history. Ultimately, buses began to replace the trolleys in the 1920s, and by the mid-thirties the trolley had disappeared from Spartanburg's streets. Service to Glendale and Clifton ceased in 1935. The car sheds and machine shops in this photograph stood on Pine Street out by Country Club Road.
Photograph courtesy of the W. S. Glenn Collection.

The wedding scene from THE WRECKER, *filmed in front of the Church of the Advent. On the groom's right is Mrs. Walter Montgomery; the groom is Tom Calvert, the bride is Beth Green, the minister is the Reverend W. H. K. Pendleton, and the little bridesmaid in the front is Peggy Gignilliat.*

Photograph courtesy of Kate M. Ward.

"The WRECKER"
A LAVISH PRODUCTION—ALL STAR CAST

A feature and a production never attempted before by amateurs in Spartanburg. Filmed and enacted successfully amid SPARTANBURG scenery by a cast of prominent people.

CAST OF "THE WRECKER"

President Calvert of the M. N. & Q. Railroad .... Arch B. Calvert
Bernard Powers Supt. of the M. N. & Q. Railroad .... J. Thos. Arnold
Mrs. Powers, his wife .... Mrs. Walter Montgomery
Helen Powers, their daughter .... Miss Beth Green
Jim Hilton, engineer on the M. N. & Q. Railroad ...... Al Montgomery
Jack Manning, engineer on the M. N. & Q. Railroad .... Tom Calvert
Board of directors—Mayor J. F. Floyd, A. M. Alexander, J. D. Garlington, I. A. Rigby, Isaac Turner, Paul E. Crosby, E. Z. White, E. C. Burnett, I. H. Greenewald, H. L. Bomar and Claude Cole.
Police Lieutenant .... W. W. Littlejohn
Police Officer .... J. B. Lee
Police Officer .... M. C. Blankenship
Fire Chief .... Chief Mitchel
Ambulance Attendant .... Romaine Dreyer
Ambulance Attendant .... W. H. Hightower
Railroad Messenger .... Windle Whitlock
Yard Clerk .... A. J. Allen
Powers' Chauffeur .... M. J. Matthews
Minister .... Rev. W. H. K. Pendleton
Best Man .... Ansel Calvert
Maid of Honor .... Miss Mary Johnson
Flower Girl .... Marguerite Thompson
Brides Maids—Miss Hattie Boyd, Miss Mary Du Pre, Miss Rachel McAully, Miss Ethel Greenewald, Miss Frances Prather, Miss Maxie Brown, and Miss Juls Calvert.
Wedding Guests—Miss Laura Chapman, Miss Annie Laura Peterson, Miss Emma Crews, Miss Ola Bush, Miss Juanita Wilkins, Miss Estelle Grant, Miss Inez Wilkins, Miss Sara Moore, Miss Constance Robertson, Miss Rosa Snowdon, Miss Carey Lindsay, Miss Anna Lear, Miss Josephine Pendleton, Mrs. E. F. Bell, Mrs. J. B. Steppe, Mrs. A. L. Mayrand, Mrs. J. M. Buckle, Mr. Paul Crosby, Mr. Rupert Alverson, Mr. Ed. Vernon, Mr. George Osborne, Mr. David Tillinghast, Mr. Robert Pendleton, Carey Pendleton and Ed. Byers.

SYNOPSIS

Jim Hilton, an engineer on the M. N. & Q. Railroad is in love with Helen Powers. One day while out automobile riding, a fire breaks out at the Rex theatre and while making a run to the fire, one of the trucks of the Spartanburg Fire Department collides with Helen's auto. Helen is rescued from the wreck by Jack Manning, also an engineer on the M. N. & Q. railroad. Of course it is a case of love at first sight between Jack and Helen. Later Jim Hilton becomes very jealous of Jack and one day and picks a quarrel with him which results in a fight. A complete knockout of one of the principals is prevented by the superintendent, Bernard Powers, arriving on the scene. President Calvert arrives in time, tardiness to inspect the Spartanburg division with the board of directors. He tells Powers to place his best engineer on the mail special as the M. N. & Q. railroad must win the mail race and hold the Government fast mail contract. Powers tells him that Jack Manning is the best engineer on the road and will make the run.

Later Jack proposes to Helen and is accepted. When Jack asks her father, Bernard Powers, for his consent to the engagement and marriage to his daughter, Powers tells him he cannot support her in her accustomed luxury on the salary of an engineer, but there is to be a race on his road for the government contract to carry Helen. Hilton hears of the coming of his rival who he will be promoted to assistant superintendent and can then marry Helen. Hilton learns of the coming mail race and of the selection of Jack to make the run. Same tempts Hilton to wreck the north and south bound trains due to pass on the double track just before Jack's engine starts the mail race. He yields to temptation and throws the switch that connects the double tracks throwing both trains on the same track. The steel monsters crash together in a head-on collision and a terrible catastrophe is revealed to our view. The scenes are of an actual wreck and at the time the pictures were taken, the fireman of one of the engines lies buried beneath his engine. This unfortunate man and turns up main delay our hero in his race for the fast mail contract, but in spite of the heavy odds he wins the race. Hilton is arrested by the crime after a spirited pistol battle on Main and Magnolia streets with the Spartanburg policemen. Later wedding bells sound when Jack and Helen are married by Rev. W. H. K. Pendleton at the Church of the Advent and leave on their honeymoon with the best wishes of their many friends attending the wedding.

SPARTAN PRINT, SPARTANBURG

In 1917 the Rex Theater featured a movie made in Spartanburg entitled THE WRECKER. The plot was a typical one in which poor boy falls in love with rich girl. When the boy asks the girl's father for permission to marry his daughter, the father tells him that he cannot support the girl in her accustomed manner. But if the boy—a crack engineer—will win the railroad race, he'll become an assistant superintendent and can marry his sweetheart. A jealous rival, wishing to cause a wreck and delay the hero, throws a switch putting both north and south bound trains on the same track. "The steel monsters crash together in a head-on collision and a terrible catastrophe is revealed to our view. The scenes are of an actual wreck and at the time the pictures were taken the fireman of one of the engines lies buried beneath his engine." So read the preview. After seeing this bloodletting, the audience witnesses a "spirited pistol battle on Main and Magnolia streets with the Spartanburg policemen." But all turns out well and our hero, who wins the race in spite of the awful delay, marries his girl in the Church of the Advent. All this for twenty cents. The show was a big hit.
Movie program courtesy of Kate M. Ward.

A Spartanburg County boy, Melvin Rhinehart, in training for the big war in 1917.

Photograph courtesy of Jennie Rhinehart.

When America entered World War I the army picked Spartanburg as a training camp for troops. In 1917, in less than a year, over nine hundred buildings were built and over twenty thousand troops were encamped a few miles west of the city. All of the buildings shown here are either officers' quarters, quartermaster buildings, offices, or other storage, processing, and medical facilites. The soldiers slept in the tents. The presence of almost 27,000 men just on the outskirts of the city proved challenging and troublesome. Prices shot up, everything became crowded, and the city began to realize in some ways what a small place it actually was. But the strain did not last long; in two years it was all over, and the camp was empty.
Photograph courtesy of the Spartanburg Herald-Journal.

117

"The Soldier must pay in suffering and death for liberty for you. What will you pay?" So was the third Liberty Loan announced and promoted in Spartanburg. The 27th Division agreed to an all-military parade along Main Street to Converse College and back again. It was the last parade in Spartanburg by the New York soldiers, and it was reviewed by the commandant of Camp Wadsworth, General John F. O'Ryan. Seven bands provided the martial music, and according to the news reports, the soldiers marched with pride and style.

Photograph courtesy of
Kate M. Ward.

The third Liberty Loan Parade of April 1918 was the occasion for this panoramic view of Spartanburg, taken by W. J. Armstrong from the roof of the Cleveland Hotel. At the extreme left is the courthouse, then the towers of Wofford College, the Cleveland Building, Central Methodist's steeple, the Andrews Building, the First Presbyterian and Baptist Church towers, and on the extreme right city hall and to its right the fire department. The Ravadson Hotel at the bottom right of the picture was primarily a boarding house for policemen and firemen.

Photograph courtesy of
R. O. and B. R. Pickens.

Movie houses began to drive out live entertainment in Spartanburg, as well as in the rest of the country, around 1910. In a few years the Bijou, the Grand, the Strand, and in 1917 the Rex all were operating on East Main Street. Of all these theaters, the Rex was the finest. In addition to special features like THE WRECKER, the Rex luridly advertised such stars as Adolphe Menjou, Conrad Nagle, and Hedda Hopper in Sinners in Silk, a 1925 feature which brought out the crowds. The interior of the Rex was photographed in the mid-twenties.

Courtesy of
Wofford College.

In 1919 there were cars on Morgan Square, but the horse-drawn buggies and wagons were slow to disappear. By this time the square had a covering of cobblestone.

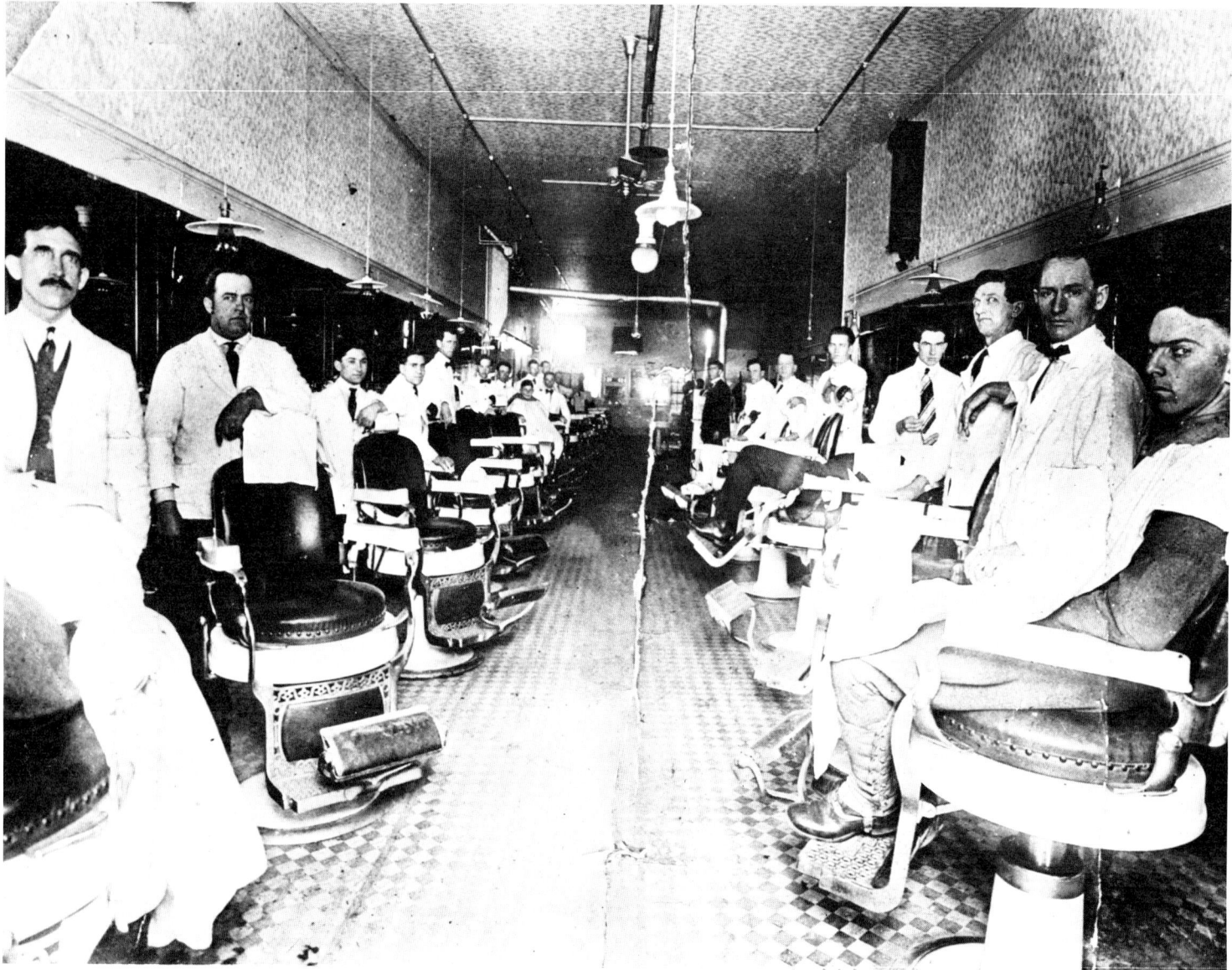

John R. Queen's Barber College on Magnolia Street, photographed around 1919. E. P. Event, a Spartanburg businessman who lived on East Main Street where Neuberger and Company is presently located, owned coal mines in Kentucky. One weekend when he was coming home from Kentucky on the train a young man sat down beside him. Wishing to engage the young man in conversation, Event asked him if he was on his way to Spartanburg. The young man replied, "Yes sir." "Do you go to school there?" asked Event. "Yes sir." "Do you have to study hard?" "Yes sir , in college we do have to study hard." "So, you attend Wofford," said Mr. Event, happy to get that settled. "Oh, no, sir; I go to Queen's Barber College."

Photograph courtesy of B & B Studio.

At 2:00 a.m. on November 11, 1918, the news of the armistice ending World War I came to Spartanburg. Immediately, Major John G. Floyd called the railways and the fire department, and whistles began to blow all over the city. People thronged to the center of town, and the celebrations continued through the next day. Here celebrants crowd around General Morgan's statue, where the Kaiser had been burned in effigy.
Photograph courtesy of the Spartanburg County Historical Association.

The victory parade wound its way up Magnolia Street. Directly across the street from the New York Restaurant was the Fairyland Theater, where the first silent movies were shown in Spartanburg. The tower on the left is the courthouse which stood where the present courthouse stands, and the building in the background which seems to be standing in the middle of the street is the Cleveland Law Range.
Photograph courtesy of the Spartanburg County Historical Association.

121

By the early 1920s automobile and truck traffic made getting around downtown dangerous. To protect pedestrians from the trucks, cars, and trolleys converging at East Main and Liberty streets, the city installed this traffic control. Patrolman William C. Gash stands at his post; at the time he was the city's sole traffic cop.

Photograph by Alfred T. Willis; courtesy of the Aug. W. Smith Company.

1920

to the Present

Immediately after World War I Spartanburg County enjoyed some boom years, but soon it was in depression. While much of the country was "roaring," Spartanburg and other cotton counties were struggling. Economic hard times came to the South much earlier than to the rest of the nation. During the twenties textiles tended to overproduce and drive prices down; despite several attempts, textile leadership in the Southeast could not organize to control production. After 1923 the trend in the industry was fewer working days, shorter hours, and less pay. As cotton prices fluctuated, generally downward, agriculture suffered. Yet, like hundreds of other cities across the nation, during the 1920s the city of Spartanburg feverishly promoted itself. The city undertook municipal projects which reflected optimism and confidence: a municipal airport, air mail service, a visit from the national hero Charles Lindbergh, a new water works, a rerouting of the Southern Railway track off East Main Street, and a new skyscraper.

Not optimism, but dogged determination marked the countryside as farmers continued to use traditional farming methods which eroded and exhausted the soil. Merchants, who risked losing money on the crop-lien system, insisted that tenants plant cotton, which was non-perishable and for which there appeared to be a market. For this reason and partly out of tradition, farmers did not diversify their crops. Yet, year after year, cotton returned less and less on the investment of time and money. The agricultural future of the county was enhanced when B. M. Bramling planted the first peaches in 1921, but it would be years before the fruit took up the slack of failing cotton prices. It would not be until after World War II that peaches would dominate the agriculture of the county.

When the depression came to the rest of the nation in 1929, the county fell apart. Many businesses closed; all six banks in the city failed by the middle of 1933, and many prominent and wealthy citizens joined the ranks of the poor. All of the problems of industry and agriculture which had existed in some form before the 1930s were magnified to catastrophe during the thirties. All of the cotton mills that did not close down during the 1930s shortened hours and lowered wages. The action worked in a fashion, for when combined with a resistance to "the dole," the number of county residents "on

In 1920 Spartanburg City Council voted to remove this fountain from Morgan Square and replace it with a drinking fountain. When John B. Cleveland gave the land known as Cleveland Park to the city in 1923, the concrete fountain was placed there. It still stands in the park, shorn of its crown of lights and converted into a gigantic planter.

relief" never rose over fourteen percent. Hundreds of mill workers who might have had reason to regret the company store in the mill village in the past, blessed it in the thirties. There was no money with which to pay employees, and mills gave out tokens redeemable at their stores. Gloom fell over the land, and at times the animosities which had long existed between town and country, management and worker, farmer and tenant exploded into bitterness and outright hostilities.

But none suffered more than Spartanburg's farmers, many of whom had resigned themselves to hopelessness. There is a belief that in hard times farmers can always get along because they can grow food. Perhaps when the soil is good such a view is justified, but during the depression many Spartanburg farms had reached a point at which they could no longer grow crops, for the land had been abused too long. For decades people grew crops on hills in vertical rows; even when some farmers sowed horizontally they did not provide for proper runoff in heavy rain. The topsoil had long ago washed away, but fertilizers introduced in the 1870s had remedied that situation and given new life to an already troubled land. In the twentieth century, as farmers grew more and more cotton without trying to deal with erosion, the land simply continued to wash away. By the thirties, huge gullies marked the farms, every road was bounded by deep crevices, and rivers and streams were filling up with sediment. In 1933 the Soil Erosion Service of the United States Department of the Interior chose Spartanburg County for its pilot erosion prevention project. By 1935, when the service was renamed the Soil Conservation Service, the department's director, Dr. Thomas S. Buie, and his associates were experimenting with erosion prevention techniques on a large scale. With the inroduction of terracing; the planting of trees, grasses, and kudzu; and the contouring of the land the county's soil came under control and began to be enriched and reclaimed for farming. No effort in the county's history has ever been so large and done so much to benefit its people. The Soil Conservation Service stopped the county from becoming a wasteland. Most green, grassy, and pine-forested areas seen about the county today were wasted, washed-out dirt patches in the late 1920s.

World War II broke the depression and brought prosperity to the nation and especially to Spartanburg. When the war department located a new training camp for troops in the county, the old problems and benefits experienced in 1917 returned. In 1941 Camp

By the early 1920s East Main Street looked somewhat less cluttered. The electrical and telephone wires had been put underground, and only the wires for the trolley cars were left. The horses, wagons, and buggies were almost all gone, and the city had installed a traffc light in the middle of East Main Street.

Photograph by Alfred T. Willis; courtesy of Nicholas Harakas.

Croft was built east of the city of Spartanburg between SC-56 and SC-176. Again, soldiers were everywhere, waiting for food and entertainment. The extra influx of money over and above the general prosperity experienced nationwide as a byproduct of the war served the ravaged economy of the area well.

After World War II Spartanburg County boomed. Its tradition of heavy investment in textiles, its selection as a proving ground for soil conservation ideas, its growing peach industry, and its aggressive leadership provided a sound basis for growth. As textiles and peaches expanded, the county's promoters sought out northern and foreign capital. In both they were successful. The influx of foreign industry and foreigners who came with it played a significant role in the cultural and economic advancement of the region.

Yet, in many ways the county continued to face age-old problems. After 1945 the accommodation of race, created and controlled by whites, was finally upset by outside pressures. Action taken by other people in other places made possible some progress by the county's black population. The forced integration of both textile mills and schools broke barriers which had seemed insurmountable a few years before. The quality of education in the county—a matter not unrelated to race prejudice—also began to eke ahead in the quarter century after 1945, with more emphasis on vocational and technical education. And the state added yet another college to Spartanburg when it opened a regional campus of the University of South Carolina here in the 1960s.

The photographs in this collection reflect a tenacious and ambitious people, a people sometimes beset with single-mindedness in agriculture and in business. The mid-twentieth century has broken that single-mindedness and diversified the use of the land and the types of industry. It has brought foreigners from abroad and from "the North," and it has brought an increasing concern with the preservation of the land and its resources. The future of the area looks bright, but in looking to the future we should not neglect its past—not because the past will teach us any lessons, but because it will give us perspective. Since the early 1800s residents of Spartanburg County have bragged about its pleasant climate and its fertile soil. They have also despaired of their poverty. But they have stayed and looked to the future. This is our legacy. We must see to it that the better parts of their world, the world of these photographs, endures.

The town of Spartanburg employed its first fireman, William Donald Mitchell, in 1897 for thirty dollars a month. The town owned two pieces of firefighting equipment: a hose and chemical wagon drawn by two horses and a steam engine drawn by three horses. When there was a fire the bell in the Opera House would toll, and the number of rings would tell the firemen in which ward the fire was burning. Strips of bacon were used to start the fire under the steam engine, and sometimes the streets were ankle deep in mud so the horses had to get to the scene of the fire as best they could. Usually by the time the steam engine got there the boiler was red hot, but often the fire was already out of control.

Lionel Lawson tells a tragic story which occurred in the same year this picture was taken, 1912. During the May Day festivities at Converse College the bell rang out for a fire in Converse Heights. The three-horse engine rushed full speed eastward on Main Street at the same time that a train was heading for the East Main Street crossing. In all the noise neither driver heard the other, and Mitchell, the driver of the fire engine, pulled hard enough on the reins to keep the wagon from colliding with the train but not soon enough to prevent the three magnificent horses from being crushed. According to Lawson the schoolchildren of the town, who had taken great pride in these beautiful horses, were deeply saddened and went by the firehouse the next day to pay their respects to the dead animals.

Saint John Street was not much more than an alley in the early 1920s. To the left of the photograph is the edge of the site of the Montgomery Building; the brick structure behind the workmen is the Southern Railway's freight depot, and just beyond it is the old Hastoc School founded in 1907. Into the 1920s the Hastoc School educated an exclusive clientele of boys under the direction of Professor Hugh T. Shockley. The upper floor had bedrooms for about twelve boarding students. A different building was used to educate girls. The academic standards of Hastoc were reputed to be very high, which was fortunate, for its location and appearance were not imposing.

Photograph by Alfred T. Willis.

127

By 1928 the Elite had developed into the epitome of the old-fashioned soda fountain.

Photograph by Alfred T. Willis; courtesy of Nicholas Harakas.

Even in 1938 some people could still afford a chauffeur. The car sits at a Gulf station with the bare fluorescent bulbs like those surrounding the bandstand in Morgan Square about 1940.

Photograph courtesy of Dexter Cleveland.

By 1940 Morgan Square had a bandstand where concerts were held every Sunday afternoon. This photograph should be compared with that of 1884. The Masonic Temple, built in 1928, stands on the far side of the Cleveland Hotel where the Opera House used to be. The Duncan Building, on the extreme right of this picture, stands where the old courthouse stood in 1884. Heinitsh Walker Drugs and Pete's Lunch (the building that has "Atlantic" painted at the top) remain to this day. The entire left side of the street has many buildings dating from the late nineteenth century, many of which still stand. All the buildings on the left, west of the Pete's Lunch block, have been torn down. The bare, fluorescent bulbs lighting the square, the presence of a filling station, and the nature of the vehicles are different, but the congestion is much the same.

Photograph courtesy of the Spartanburg Herald-Journal.

Polly Anderson sits for her portrait at the county fair in 1940. The moon was an actual seat. More than anything else this picture captures the innocence and fun of a county fair.

Photograph courtesy of Jennie Rhinehart.

By the late 1930s and early 1940s, when this photograph was taken, the county fair had replaced harness racing with automobile racing.

Photograph by Alfred T. Willis; courtesy of the Piedmont Interstate Fair Association.

While Aug. W. Smith's windows were usually interesting, James Buchanan always did something special for Christmas. Here is one of his designs on the marquee for a Christmas in the early 1930s. Buchanan made everything in his displays by hand with thimbles, needles, thread, and anything else he could get hold of. Buchanan was also a photographer—many of his photographs appear in the early pages of this book—and eventual caretaker of Walnut Grove, the eighteenth-century residence of Charles Moore.

Photograph courtesy of the Aug. W. Smith Company.

By mid-century moviegoing was the chief form of entertainment for youngsters on a Saturday afternoon.
Photograph courtesy of B & B Studio.

For other audiences entertainment could be found at Converse, where recitals were held throughout the academic year; at Wofford, where the Glee Club entertained hundreds; and at the annual Music Festival. This is a festival audience in the early 1940s.
Photograph courtesy of Converse College.

Around mid-century there were three great fires that changed the look of the downtown area. This one took place at the Leader department store in the early forties. Two others occurred in the 1960s: the First Baptist Church and the old Elite which had become a cafeteria.

Photograph courtesy of B & B Studio.

The Morgans leave their farm with all their worldly possessions, a not-uncommon site in the thirties and forties.

Photograph courtesy of
Pat McKinney.

167

For Harley Morgan of Woodruff, having to abandon another farm was simply part of his life. It had happened to him before, and as far as he knew it might happen again. The difference this time, though, was that he was leaving a farm which was badly eroded for one that had been reclaimed by the Soil Conservation Service. His new home would be the first for the Morgans with electric lights. He moved in 1941.

Photograph courtesy of the South Carolina Museum Commission.

In spite of the heroic efforts of the Soil Conservation Service, farms were being abandoned throughout the 1940s. Dejected farm families moved on, to what they often did not know; what they did know was that their land could do no more for them. This abandoned farm house, typical of hundreds in the county, was photographed in 1946.

Courtesy of the South Carolina Museum Commission.

The Soil Conservation Service introduced Spartanburg County farmers to many alternative ways of preventing erosion. This 1941 photograph of Fernwood Orchard illustrates contour planting and strip cropping as well as the planting of various grains to hold the soil. In the background on the left is a kudzu meadow strip. Running along the top of the photograph is Highway 29, and the road running from top left to bottom right is Fernwood Drive.

Photograph courtesy of Pat McKinney.

Lord Lothian's telegram.

Courtesy of
Converse College.

In 1940 Britain was under heavy attack by Hitler's military machine. Sympathy for the English was growing quickly in the United States, although the government seemed to many to be moving pitifully slow in rendering aid. The Americans were supposed to be neutral, but by late 1940 it was abundantly clear where their sympathies lay. There were many private efforts to help the British people, the major relief organization being Bundles for Britain. On December 6, 1940, the Spartanburg Lyric Opera Company presented a production of The Gondoliers for the benefit of Bundles for Britain. People from around the county, students from Converse, Wofford, and Spartanburg High School plus the Union High School band all took part in the production. It was a triumph; the audience numbered about 1,500, and they were treated to a telegram of thanks from the popular British ambassador to the United States, Lord Lothian. The telegram was read to the audience by Ernst Bacon, who directed the production. The thrill of the triumph was marred somewhat in the next few weeks when Lord Lothian, who had worked so hard and successfully to get help for his government from the Americans, died in Washington.

Photograph courtesy of
Converse College.

170

Three Spartanburg County GIs show typical American cockiness somewhere in Europe in 1944. From left to right: Orville Kirby, J. E. Hodge, and Joe Varner.

Photograph courtesy of Don Camby.

Providing entertainment for the thousands of men passing through Camp Croft was a formidable task. A USO was established in Spartanburg, and artists of all kinds came to the camp itself to entertain the troops. Residents of the county were welcome to visit the camp on these occasions, and this welcome gave many people the opportunity to enjoy entertainers they otherwise would never have seen.

Photograph courtesy of the Spartanburg Herald-Journal.

These troops are learning techniques for attacking and defending villages in the fighting course located at Camp Croft.

Photograph courtesy of the Spartanburg Herald-Journal.

171

In the early 1940s people turned out to greet one of the many performers who had come to entertain the troops at Camp Croft and at the local USO. Note the USO sign at the bottom of the photograph. By mid-century, city leaders decided that Daniel Morgan Square had to be reorganized to alleviate traffic congestion on Church Street and around the Daniel Morgan monument at the intersection of Main and Magnolia streets. As part of the reorganization the buildings directly behind the crowd on the left were torn down, the eastern half of the building housing Greenewald's was destroyed, and Daniel Morgan was moved to the spot where he stands now in front of Greenewald's.

Photograph courtesy of the Spartanburg Herald-Journal.

The Army Signal Corps made this aerial photograph of Camp Croft in the early 1940s. In 1940 the war department bought a 22,000-acre tract between SC-56 and SC-176 southeast of the city of Spartanburg for the basic training of infantry troops. In February 1941 the United States Army activated Camp Croft, named for South Carolina-born Major General Edward Croft. From eighteen to twenty thousand men were trained at the facility every three months. At the end of the war, the war department decided not to make the camp a permanent military base. The Spartanburg County Foundation bought it for more than one million dollars in March 1945; the foundation has authority to dispose of the property in any way it wishes, the proceeds to benefit the county. Most of the land has been sold for industrial use.

Photograph courtesy of the Spartanburg Herald-Journal.

For some soldiers, fun was not the only interest pursued in their meager time off. Many attended special classes at the local colleges. Here a group of soldiers are at Converse; perhaps the fact that the college was for women did not hurt enrollment.

Photograph courtesy of Converse College.

172

In the fall of 1942 Spartanburg's cotton growers faced disaster. The cotton crop was a large one and was ready to be picked, but the war had so depleted manpower that the farmers could not possibly pick the crop by themselves. So on October 8 all students in Spartanburg County were excused from classes to go out and pick cotton. Both Converse and Wofford students joined the pickers. Here some Wofford students are hard at work alongside Dr. Clarence Norton, Wofford's dean of students, and to his left Charles P. Hammond of Hammond, Brown, Jennings' furniture store.

Approximately three hundred students picked fifteen thousand pounds of cotton in that one day. Both this effort and the Bundles for Britain project demonstrate the county's community spirit and patriotism during the war years.

Photograph courtesy of Pat McKinney.

Converse students pick cotton in 1942.
Photograph courtesy of Converse College.

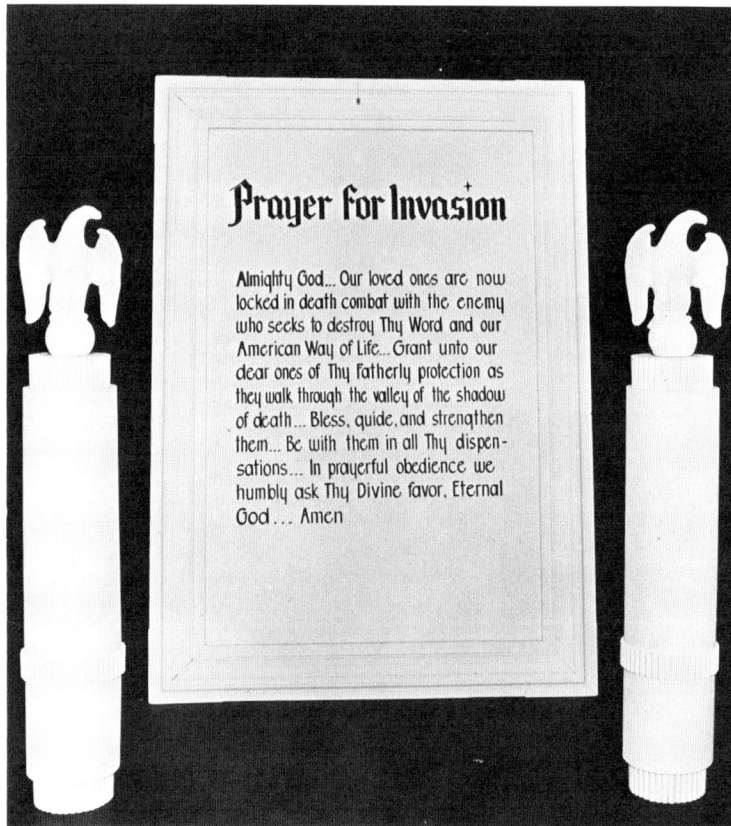

Prayer for Invasion

Almighty God... Our loved ones are now locked in death combat with the enemy who seeks to destroy Thy Word and our American Way of Life... Grant unto our dear ones of Thy Fatherly protection as they walk through the valley of the shadow of death... Bless, guide, and strengthen them... Be with them in all Thy dispensations... In prayerful obedience we humbly ask Thy Divine favor, Eternal God... Amen

Harry Smiley, who arranged for Rabbi Wrubel of Temple B'nai Israel in Spartanburg to prepare this prayer, made this display far in advance for the day when Allied forces should invade Europe. When news of the invasion, which had begun at 3:23 p.m. on June 6, 1944, was flashed, Smiley set his alarm for five o'clock the next morning and had the display ready at six. In the following weeks hundreds stopped, read the prayer, and wept.

Photograph courtesy of the Aug. W. Smith Company.

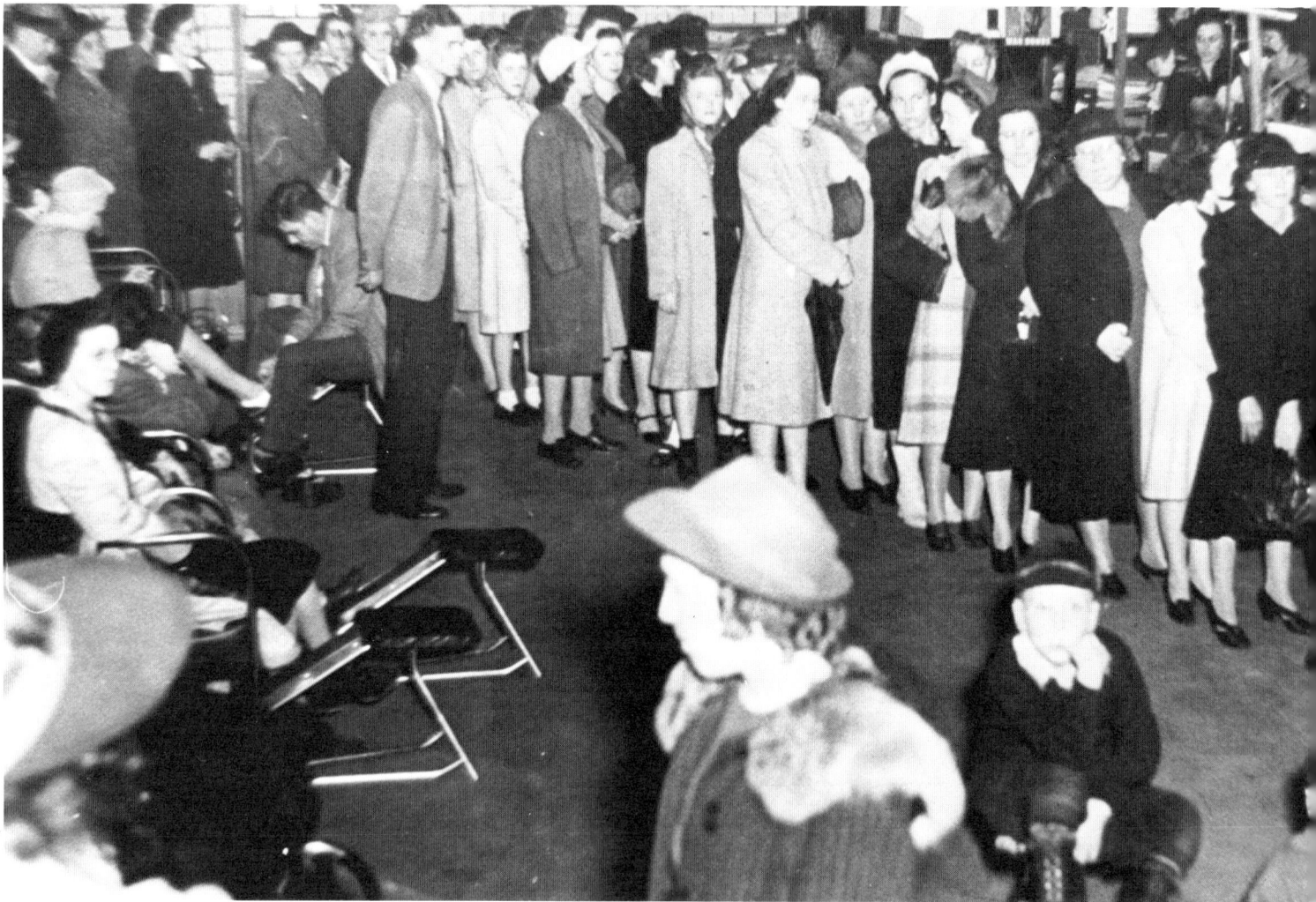

The site of Memorial Auditorium on North Chruch Street looked like this in 1945. The cottage house in the center is typical of mid-twentieth century housing in the city.
Photograph by Alfred T. Willis; courtesy of the Aug. W. Smith Company.

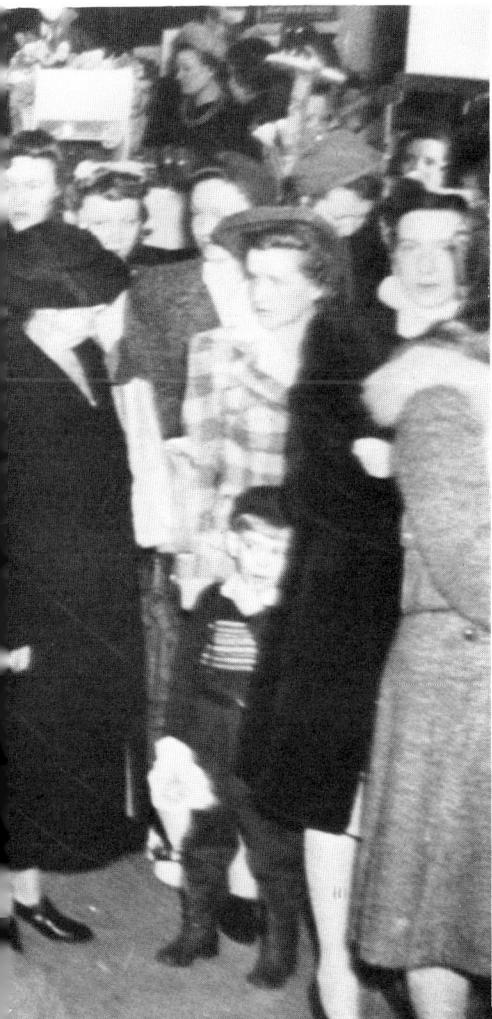

During World War II nylons were almost impossible to obtain. When Aug. W. Smith announced a sale on them in 1943 more than six hundred women crowded the store. In twenty minutes the nylons were gone, but the store brought out two hundred pair of silk hose it had set aside for the following week so the customers would not be too disappointed.
Photograph by Kathryn Powell; courtesy of the Aug. W. Smith Company.

Jalopies and hot rods occupied much of the attention of young men during the forties and fifties. Here Carlos Anderson shows off his "wheels."
Photograph courtesy of Jennie Rhinehart.

This is what a formal ball looked like at the Cleveland Hotel in the mid-forties.
Photograph courtesy of Dexter Cleveland.

The annual Christmas parade has long been a favorite event for local youngsters. In 1949 the Aug. W. Smith Company provided this float of the "old woman in the shoe." When the float passed by Wofford College the low limbs which hung over North Church Street at that time tore the top from the shoe.

Photograph courtesy of the Aug. W. Smith Company.

In the late 1940s the Elite had changed into a full-fledged restaurant with live entertainment—in this case a blind piano player.

Photograph in the Willis Collection; courtesy of Nicholas Harakas.

This view of Main Street from the corner of Liberty looking toward Morgan Square was taken in the late 1940s. It must have been a Saturday afternoon, for the Palmetto is featuring *Wild Bill Hickok Rides* plus *Superman* cartoons, and bicycles are parked in front of both the Palmetto and the Strand theaters.

Photograph courtesy of the Spartanburg Herald-Journal.

Although by the 1940s Magnolia, East Main, and Pine streets had already lost or were about to lose most of their old homes, other old houses managed to survive. For better or worse, many such as Bonhaven underwent "face lifts" in an effort to achieve "the look" of a younger (newer) era. This is a photograph of Bonhaven after renovation; the original structure appears earlier in this book.

Photograph courtesy of Dexter Cleveland.

After the war the peach industry flourished. These photographs were taken in the 1950s at Paul Black's peach orchards. Here the peaches are being brought in from the fields for processing.

Photograph by Ruth Gilman; courtesy of Marianna Black Habisreutinger.

179

These women are grading the peaches which will then be washed and brushed by machines; it's called "defuzzing."

Photograph courtesy of Marianna Black Habisreutinger.

Finally the peaches are put into baskets. These people are arranging the nicest peaches in shallow round trays which will be placed on top of the basket to give it a finished and pretty look. This process is called "ringing." The baskets then are loaded into the boxcars on the right for shipment.

Photograph courtesy of Marianna Black Habisreutinger.

181

In 1956 East Main Street from the corner of Pine Street going toward Converse was still residential, and the commerical buildings which now line both sides of the street were in the future.

Photograph courtesy of Jesse Franklin Cleveland.

This photograph was taken in 1956 at the corner of Pine and East Main streets looking north on Pine. North Pine Street had not been built into a proper street as yet. On the left now stands the First National Bank and on the right the Cabana Restaurant.

Photograph courtesy of Jesse Franklin Cleveland.

Before the coming of suburban shopping centers, East Main Street looked like this from the corner of Church in 1957. The Main Street Mall now occupies this space.

Photograph courtesy of Wofford College.

The manufacturers in the county had segregated baseball teams well past mid-century. This is the Draper black baseball team in 1954.

Photograph courtesy of the Charlie Mae Campbell family.

In order to ease traffic congestion in downtown Spartanburg, in 1960 city officials decided to move the statue of General Daniel Morgan from its location in the middle of Morgan Square opposite Magnolia Street to its present location on the east end of the square. To continue to face the general in his traditional direction—northwest—would be to have him look directly into the building on the east side of North Church Street, so it was decided to turn him around and have him face out over the square in a southeastward direction. It seemed bad enough to many old-time Spartanburg residents to move the general at all, but to have him face southward, as if he expected enemies to come from that direction, was even more unsettling. One resident summed up the feelings of many: "The general would not approve!" Nevertheless, the change was made in September 1960. This photograph shows Morgan being lowered from his pedestal in the middle of the square. The tall building to the left of the pedestal is the Andrews Building, now destroyed.

Photograph courtesy of B & B Studio.

In 1962 the First Baptist Church burned. The landmark had stood on the corner of Dean and East Main streets for more than half a century. The new church was built soon after on the same site.
Photograph courtesy of B & B Studio.

In many ways it appears that the Southeast, and Spartanburg County in particular, has a bright future. When contemplating that future, however, it would be well to remember that few people in the county live in grand houses like those that appear at the front of this book. Some people continue to live in houses like this one.
Photograph by Linda Taylor Hudgins.

In 1946 the Piedmont Interstate Fair Association was organized to replace and enlarge the old county fair. The purpose of the new organization was to combine the efforts of six counties (Laurens, Polk, Rutherford, Cherokee, Union, and Spartanburg) to better show off their industrial and agricultural potential. In 1947 Paul Black was elected president of the Fair Association and served in that capacity until his death in 1975. The Interstate Fair built a concrete grandstand in 1956 to replace the old wooden structure, and harness racing was replaced by stock car racing—the highlight of the week's activities. When the carnival performers used to arrive by train, people would flock to the station on the Sunday before fair week to watch as the animals and performers disembarked. Since just after the turn of the century, fair week in Spartanburg has been an exciting time, and it is one of the county's oldest traditions.
Photograph courtesy of the Piedmont Interstate Fair Association.

All over America in the 1960s suburban shopping centers drew shoppers away from the traditional downtown stores. As business in the center of town declined, city officials and downtown merchants banded together "to save downtown." Salvation would come by way of creating malls in the center city with convenient offstreet parking and inviting atmosphere in which to spend a few hours. The city of Spartanburg suffered from the same problems as other towns and sought her solutions in the same way. The Main Street Mall, dedicated in 1974, stretches from Converse Street to Church Street.

Photograph courtesy of B & B Studio.

Ever since 1884, when Seth Milliken negotiated to become the selling agent for the Pacolet Manufacturing Company, the Milliken name has been an important one in the county. This reseach facility was opened in 1958.
Photograph courtesy of Milliken and Company.

Hoechst Fibers Industries, a division of American Hoechst Corporation, began as a joint venture between an American firm and Farbwerke Hoechst AG of Frankfurt, West Germany. Located on a 670-acre site at I-85, it employs approximately 2,200 persons.

Photograph by Lavoy Studio; courtesy of Hoechst Fibers Industries.

As Spartanburg County grows and
prospers in the last half of the
twentieth century, its physical character
is constantly changing. It appears that
the impact of those changes on the
look of the area will match that of the
turn of the century. Among the finer
examples of the new architecture in the
region is the Sandor Teszler Library at
Wofford College, constructed in 1969.

Photograph by Mark Olencki;
courtesy of Wofford College.

Sales day in Morgan Square.
Nineteenth century photograph
from the Willis Collection;
courtesy of the Aug. W. Smith
Company.

ABOUT THE AUTHOR: Philip N. Racine is Associate Professor of History at Wofford College. He holds an A.B. from Bowdoin College and an M.A. and Ph.D. from Emory University. Author of many scholarly articles, Dr. Racine has long had a personal interest in regional history. A native of Maine, he and his family have lived in Spartanburg since 1969.